WALI

WEST
M

Paul Hannon

HILLSIDE

HILLSIDE GUIDES - ACROSS THE NORTH

Long Distance Walks
•COAST TO COAST WALK   •DALES WAY   •CLEVELAND WAY
•WESTMORLAND WAY   •FURNESS WAY   •CUMBERLAND WAY
•PENDLE WAY •LADY ANNE'S WAY •NORTH BOWLAND TRAVERSE

Circular Walks - Lancashire
•BOWLAND   •PENDLE & THE RIBBLE   •WEST PENNINE MOORS

Circular Walks - Yorkshire Dales
•HOWGILL FELLS   •THREE PEAKS   •MALHAMDALE
•WHARFEDALE   •NIDDERDALE   •WENSLEYDALE   •SWALEDALE

Circular Walks - North York Moors
•WESTERN MOORS   •SOUTHERN MOORS   •NORTHERN MOORS

Circular Walks - South Pennines
•BRONTE COUNTRY   •CALDERDALE   •ILKLEY MOOR

Circular Walks - Peak District
•EASTERN PEAK   •NORTHERN PEAK   •CENTRAL PEAK
•SOUTHERN PEAK   •WESTERN PEAK

Circular Walks - North Pennines
•TEESDALE   •EDEN VALLEY

Hillwalking - Lake District
•OVER LAKELAND MOUNTAINS   •OVER LAKELAND FELLS

Yorkshire Pub Walks
•HARROGATE/WHARFE VALLEY   •HAWORTH/AIRE VALLEY

Large format colour hardback

FREEDOM OF THE DALES

BIKING COUNTRY
•YORKSHIRE DALES CYCLE WAY   •WEST YORKSHIRE CYCLE WAY
•MOUNTAIN BIKING - WEST & SOUTH YORKSHIRE
•AIRE VALLEY BIKING GUIDE   •CALDERDALE BIKING GUIDE
• GLASGOW Clyde Valley & Loch Lomond

• YORK WALKS *City Theme Walks*

•WALKING COUNTRY TRIVIA QUIZ *Over 1000 questions*

Please write for latest details and prices

WALKING COUNTRY

WEST PENNINE MOORS

Paul Hannon

HILLSIDE

HILLSIDE
PUBLICATIONS
11 Nessfield Grove
Keighley
West Yorkshire
BD22 6NU

First published in 1998

© Paul Hannon 1998

ISBN 1 870141 59 8

Cover illustrations:
Rivington Pike; Darwen Tower
Back cover: Anglezarke from the Pigeon Tower;
The Black Dog, Belmont; Great Hill from Darwen Hill;
Rivington Tower to Winter Hill
(Paul Hannon/Big Country Picture Library)

Page 1: Great House Barn, Rivington;
Page 3: Guidepost, Darwen Moor

Printed in Great Britain by
Carnmor Print and Design
95-97 London Road
Preston
Lancashire
PR1 4BA

CONTENTS

INTRODUCTION

The West Pennine Moors is a designated recreational area in the heart of Lancashire. It extends to 90 square miles, comprising of moorland, valleys, wooded cloughs, forestry, farmland and reservoirs. The area is fringed by main roads linking the bustling towns of Blackburn, Accrington, Darwen, Rawtenstall, Bury, Bolton, Horwich and Chorley.

A West Pennine Moors Area Management Committee has responsibility for the area, including its Ranger and Information services. The Countryside Service is funded by Lancashire County Council, North West Water, Bury Metro, Bolton Metro and the Countryside Commission. It currently operates four information centres at the most popular parts of the area, and any of these makes an ideal first stop for visitors. As opening times can vary these have not been given, this also applies to several other attractions passed on these walks.

These 22 walks embrace a wide geographical spread, each featuring numerous places of interest. Outstanding architecture is found at Turton Tower and Smithills Hall: other absorbing buildings include Rivington Barns and Helmshore Textile Museum. Industrial archaeology is sampled at Lead Mines Clough, Anglezarke, and Broadhead Clough coke ovens. There are many signs of small-scale quarrying and collieries on the moors, and views to not so distant mill chimneys. Abandoned industrial hamlets like White Coppice and Barrow Bridge now form characterful backwaters. There is evidence of early man on the moors at Cheetham Close and Noon Hill: though there is nothing dramatic, Round Loaf is a real gem. Splendid woodland is found at Roddlesworth, Sunnyhurst and Lever Park, while there is relaxing reservoir walking at Entwistle, Anglezarke and Haslingden Grane.

The area's crowning glory is its windswept and often lonely heights, Winter Hill, Bull Hill and Great Hill supported by the likes of Turton Moor, Darwen Moor and Haslingden Moor. Fascinating side valleys abound, as at Musbury and Longworth Cloughs and Smithills Dean. Oswaldtwistle Moor, Grey Stone Hill and Anglezarke Moor offer bleaker surrounds. The moors bear numerous adornments as man has attempted to strengthen their identity, the stone towers on Darwen Moor, Holcombe Moor and at Rivington having been joined by the less appealing array of masts on Winter Hill. While the sight and sound of industry and urbanisation may never be far away, it will usually seem like it is once you set foot on the West Pennine Moors.

6

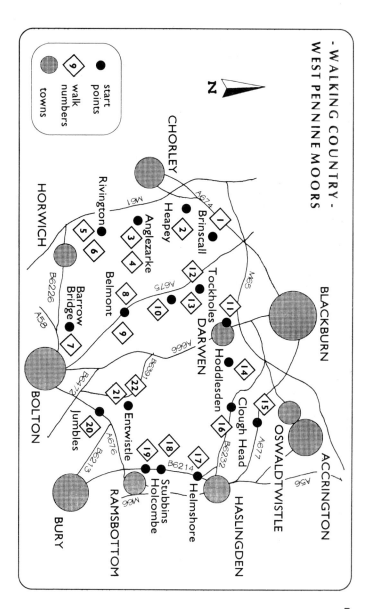

- WALKING COUNTRY -
WEST PENNINE MOORS

N

●	start points
◇ 9	walk numbers
▨	towns

CHORLEY

HORWICH

Rivington

Heapey

Brinscall

Anglezarke

Belmont

Barrow Bridge

Tockholes

DARWEN

Hoddlesden

BLACKBURN

Clough Head

OSWALDTWISTLE

ACCRINGTON

Entwistle

Jumbles

BOLTON

Stubbins
Holcombe

Helmshore

HASLINGDEN

RAMSBOTTOM

BURY

M61

A674

M65

A675

A666

B6226

A58

B6391

B6472

B6213

A676

M66

B6214

B6232

A677

A56

7

Access

All the walks follow rights of way, concession or other accepted paths, or are on National Trust or other access land. A large tract of the higher moors is subject to an access agreement between the local authorities and landowners. This area is clearly indicated on the West Pennine Moors Explorer map by a purple line. The area should only be entered at recognised access points, where gates and stiles are provided: many of these are where rights of way enter the area. Once within the area the walker is free to roam at will, subject to the relevant bye-laws.

The area can be closed at times of high fire risk (this might provoke ironic laughter from cagoule-clad, swamp-squelching ramblers, but moorland fires have in fact wreaked havoc). Additionally, part of the area above Belmont can be closed for several days a year for 'sporting' purposes, though none of the walks in this book cross that particular corner (the rights of way are of course always open). Indeed, most of the walks that take in the access area do in any case stick to recognised paths, leaving suitably equipped and experienced walkers to break off and do their own thing as and when desired.

Other areas of public access on foot include Darwen Moor, an urban common; and Holcombe Moor, in the hands of the National Trust. Parts of Holcombe Moor are within the hands of a very different body to the NT, namely the MOD. The moorland including Bull Hill is within a Ministry of Defence firing range, and can be closed to the public when in use: and this does include the rights of way. Only Walk 18 passes through this area, while Walk 19 has an optional detour within it. The Range Liaison Officer can be contacted on 01204-882770 to ascertain if firing is to take place (the boundaries of the range are marked by warning posts, and red flags fly when the range is in use).

The Country Code
- Respect the life and work of the countryside
- Protect wildlife, plants and trees
- Keep to public paths across farmland
- Safeguard water supplies • Go carefully on country roads
- Keep dogs under control • Guard against all risks of fire
- Fasten all gates • Leave no litter - take it with you
- Make no unnecessary noise
- Leave livestock, crops and machinery alone
- Use gates and stiles to cross fences, hedges and walls

Getting around

All the walks start from either designated car parks or places with other adequate parking. Additionally, almost every walk is on or near a bus (or sometimes train) route, and this is indicated at the start of each walk. Public transport across the area is largely very good, as would be expected of a country area surrounded by large towns. Buses run along most of the main roads, and also serve some of the villages such as Tockholes and Hoddlesden. The Blackburn-Bolton railway runs through the very centre of the area, with stations at Darwen, Entwistle and Bromley Cross, and other lines serve the fringes to north and west. With a little planning, various permutations can be created by linking different sections of the walks, to create longer routes or to take advantage of public transport.

Using the guide

Each walk is self-contained, with essential information being followed by a simple map and concise description of the route. Dovetailed between this are useful notes of features along the way, and interspersed are illustrations which both capture the flavour of the walks and record many of the items of interest. In order to make the instructions easier to follow, essential route description has been highlighted in bold type, while items in lighter type refer to historical asides and things to look out for: in this format you can find your way more easily while still locating features of interest at the relevant point in the text.

The simple sketch maps identify the location of the routes rather than the fine detail, and whilst the route description should be sufficient to guide you around, an Ordnance Survey map is recommended: the route can easily be plotted on the relevant OS map. To gain the most from a walk, the detail of the 1:25,000 maps is unsurpassed. They also serve to vary walks as desired, giving an improved picture of one's surroundings and the availability of linking paths. Just one map covers every single walk in the book:-

• *Explorer Sheet 19 - West Pennine Moors*

Please note that as Explorer maps to the surrounding area are published (around the year 2000), this sheet number will be amended.

Also extremely useful for general planning purposes are the Landranger maps at 1:50,000, and two sheets cover the area:

103, Blackburn & Burnley
109, Manchester

GREAT HILL

START *Brinscall*   *Grid ref. SD 628214*

DISTANCE *6½ miles*

ORDNANCE SURVEY MAPS
1:50,000
Landranger 103 - Blackburn & Burnley; Landranger 109 - Manchester
1:25,000
Explorer 19 - West Pennine Moors

ACCESS *Start from the junction of School Lane and Railway Road, at a sharp bend of the road at the eastern end of the village. There is street parking here, or a small parking area on Quarry Road, on the side road just off the junction (by St. Luke's church). Served by bus from Chorley and Blackburn.*

A bracing stroll through a variety of country before the climb to the walk's objective. The first section is of necessity rather weighty with route description.

❺ Leave the junction by the side road over the Goit. This was built to carry water from the Roddlesworth reservoirs (see WALK 12) to Rivington. **With Quarry Road on the left (note the stone trough), turn right up Well Lane.** An easy option is simply to head up the lane, but within a minute there is the chance for an early variation, which rejoins the lane a little higher.

At an access notice a path runs along into the woods on the right. Maintain this level course for a lovely woodland walk until an abrupt halt at a steep-sided stream. Here the path turns sharp left with it. A low level branch then runs close by the stream, into the broad amphitheatre of a former quarry. Upstream is a fine prospect of a waterfall which can soon be better seen. As the right of way is an

impasse, resume on a higher-level, thin path above the steep bank. This gains height with the waterfall and earns a good view of it before being nudged to cross a fence (makeshift stile) back onto Well Lane.

Those remaining on Well Lane will see the variation rejoin as a rough road just above a waterfall: the walk will return to this point at its conclusion. For now, resume up Well Lane for just a further 100 yards or so and take a stile on the left. A green track rises to an old gateway at the foot of rough moorland. Though the track swings left, our fainter way bears right, rising with an old wall. The thin path rises through another old wall and up the moor edge, a wall rejoining us to rise to a corner with an old barn to the right: by this point the path has faded away. Also by now, there is a good prospect of the Bowland moors to the north, and also west over the plain.

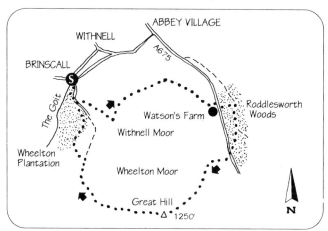

From the corner stile rise again, a wall soon joining the now clear green track. This rises to sturdy gateposts with the remains of Solomon's Temple to the right. The ruin makes a sad scene at the upper limits of the green pastures. Approaching it, Darwen Tower has made its appearance on the skyline to the left. Up ahead, the cairn on Great Hill can be seen, though it will be some time yet before we're stood by it. At the gateposts double back left on a clear green path across the rough moor, aiming broadly in the direction of Darwen Tower. At an old wall the path passes through two more gateposts and starts to descend through heather.

Within thirty yards the path forks, bear right on the clearer branch which runs across to intercept a broad grassy track at a cairn. Cross straight over, now pathless as we head on through an old wall and improving moorland to the brow. This is Millstone Edge, where a few stones repose. Note the forlorn condition of all the field walls ahead. Drop down to arrive above a side stream. Angle right a little to drop to a natural crossing point, with a step-stile in the fence behind.

Head directly away to the foot of an old walled green way. Keep straight on with the old wall to the far corner, where a tractor track is met. Turn right on this to be briefly enclosed by old walls. Emerging, leave the track and bear left along the wall-side. This leads to a ladder-stile into the head of a plantation, with another out of it just beyond. Rise past some low ruins and through a wall-gap to a stile and gateway above. Darwen Tower remains in view ahead throughout this section. A grassy track passes a wall corner and on to another in the far corner. Aided by a line of telephone wires, bear gently right and on to a gate with a line of trees either side. A farm appears ahead and the track leads unfailingly there. In the yard bear left on the short drive out onto the A675 Preston-Bolton road.

A few yards to the right a sign points a thin path into Roddlesworth Woods, gently declining to meet a rough road at Rocky Brook, more properly the river Roddlesworth. This junction of many ways is a lovely spot in the heart of the woods. Turn right over Halliwell Fold Bridge and head upstream on the broad track, rising gently above a steep bank above the brook. On easing out, leave it by a grassy path angling gently towards the stream, past the site of old quarries. This soon runs upstream to a delightful waterfall. The now broader way and stream lead to a concrete footbridge at a lovely watersmeet. Cross and take the right branch up to the road at Calf Hey Bridge.

Great Hill awaits ahead, a stark contrast of open moorland after the woods. Go briefly left on the road, then take the thin path off to the right to a stile onto the moor. A good path heads away between fence and stream. This runs circuitously round to a bend where it crosses both stream and wall, and runs to the ruins of Pimms beneath a stand of four windswept sycamores. Beyond it the path climbs steeper before easing out at some low ruins, and then on broader ground to the summit of Great Hill. A sprawling cairn in the peat marks this fine vantage point, at 1250ft/381m the summit of the walk. Much work during 1997 saw the laying of old flagstones on this tired path. Winter

Hill and Rivington Pike dominate to the south, but the finest features are northwards, where green pastures lead the eye to an uninterrupted array of the Bowland moors. Around to the right is Pendle Hill, and on a clear day the peaks of the Yorkshire Dales slot in behind.

Resume westwards on the quickly improving path which tramps the distinctive edge. Dropping off it, both the terrain and the path broaden to arrive at the remains of Drinkwaters. Just past here a brass plaque in the track-side wall indicates the presence of Joe's Cup, a well just under the track. **Head away past a small belt of trees to a 1963 Ramblers' Association guidepost marking a fork of paths. Our way remains on the broad track, swinging round to the right and running a largely level course, enjoying easy strides with Bowland returning to add interest ahead. After flirting with an old wall, a sturdy one is met at a corner after a pronounced kink. Forsake the track and take the contrastingly inviting thin path down the wall-side to a corner of the moor. Through an old gateway, the part-sunken path slants down to a small quarry, then down to a stile into the trees.**

Turn sharp right on a path which runs a splendid course along the top of the wood. Early on we pass through the lichen- and bracken-covered remains of Liptrot's Farm, while the heather moor remains just over the wall. **When the wall turns off right, our path runs left, descending to merge into a broader track. Bear right on this to drop down to meet the road of yore at the bridge above the waterfall. Rejoin Well Lane and head down it for the final five minutes.**

The summit of Great Hill, looking to Darwen Tower

2

WHITE COPPICE

START Heapey   Grid ref. SD 610197

DISTANCE 4¾ miles

ORDNANCE SURVEY MAPS
1:50,000
Landranger 109 - Manchester
1:25,000
Explorer 19 - West Pennine Moors

ACCESS Start from the Railway pub at the junction of Chapel Lane, Tithebarn Lane and Coppice Lane on the way to White Coppice. Reached from either the A674 Chorley-Blackburn road at Wheelton or Heapey Road off the B6228 out of Chorley. Roadside parking on Coppice Lane. Nearest buses: Chorley, Wheelton and Brinscall. An alternative start is Higher House Lane car park, just off Heapey Road off the B6228 out of Chorley. • ACCESS AREA - see page 8.

An utterly delightful stroll visiting the viewpoints of Healey Nab and Stronstrey Bank, and innumerable tiny reservoirs. White Coppice alone is worth the walk. There is the added bonus of options to create smaller alternative routes.

S Descend Coppice Lane from the pub, in the direction of White Coppice. Passing above the former Blackburn-Chorley railway line, at the first opportunity take a path signposted through Causeway House Farm on the right. A short descent is made to a small embankment dividing two reservoirs. It is to this attractive corner the walk will return, so for now turn right on a broad grassy path along the southern shore of the larger reservoir. At the far end advance straight on (glimpsing a third reservoir on the right) to enter a car park, and out onto Higher House Lane. Ahead is modern housing where green fields were.

Turn left up the lane, and around the corner past Moody House Farm (Mouldy House on the map) to reach a sharp bend. Here go straight ahead on the short drive to Higher Healey. The track is deflected to the right outside the grounds. A glimpse of the main house reveals some mullioned and transomed windows. At the end advance along the main, central track, a pleasant enclosed green way. In front looms the gentle wooded knoll of Healey Nab. There are big views over to the right beyond the buzz of the M61 motorway (little more than half a mile away at this point) and Chorley to Harrock Hill. The track emerges onto an open bank and rises to enter the wood.

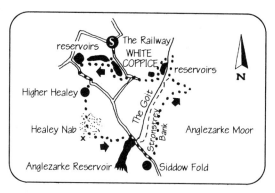

A few yards into the trees is a major fork, both being concession bridleways. Take the right branch, dropping slightly and running pleasantly on to quickly reach another fork. This time opt for the broad pathway slanting to the left, soon reaching the edge of the wood atop Healey Nab. It then climbs by the wallside to the brow of the hill. A well used path runs the few yards to the open top where a scrappy cairn occupies a more substantial ruined base. At a modest 672ft/205m the views are extensive, the earlier features now usurped by the scene to the east, where Stronstrey Bank's colourful flank is overtopped by Anglezarke Moor with Winter Hill beyond.

Paths lead down either side of the wall to the bottom corner of the wood. Go straight ahead to a path crossroads in this open scrubby heath, not quite in sequence with the map. Turn right on the broader path, which winds round past old, small scale quarry workings to drop down to a junction with a level bridleway. Go right just a few yards and take a stile on the left. Slant left down the field to a ladder-stile in the bottom corner, from where a stepped path spirals down the beech wooded bank to rejoin Higher House Lane at the corner of Anglezarke Reservoir.

Cross the road over the reservoir head. This affords good views down the length of what is by far the largest of the walk's reservoirs. **Follow the road away past Waterman's Cottage, an isolated house built by Liverpool Corporation in the 1850s.** A kissing-gate on the left gives entry to the access area, and the option of a low level return: simply follow the broad track which swings left along the base of Stronstrey Bank to arrive at a stone bridge over the Goit at White Coppice. **For the full itinerary, remain on Moor Road as it climbs steeply alongside colourful scrubby woodland. At the top, Siddow Fold, to the right, bears a 1707 datestone. Take a stile on the left onto open moor, and a faint path heads away with the fence, rising gradually into the heather.** Looking back, Anglezarke Reservoir is seen to advantage.

At the fence corner a similarly thin path is joined and followed left along the moor edge, still in the company of the fence. Though the fence precludes dramatic views over the edge of Stronstrey Bank, this is nevertheless a grand stride on a good heather path. Of particular relevance in the view are Healey Nab and the first string of reservoirs. **Towards the end the path drops slightly to a crumbling wall. Bear gently right to pass through a gap, and on through scattered rocks to rejoin the fence overlooking the sheer walls of an old quarry.** A near bird's-eye view of White Coppice features the cricket pitch nestling in the folds of the hills, attended by more small reservoirs. It is clear why this is claimed to be the most attractively sited pitch in the county.

Resume with the fence until it drops away after a second quarry site. An option here is to drop steeply with it to gain the track in the valley floor, but better to remain on the well defined edge, a thin trod leading on to the deep defile of the clough of Dean Black Brook. Approach with caution as the steep walls of another old quarry line the clough. Instead bear round to the right, and maintaining the contour, walk upstream above the clough. Immediately below us its steep rocky walls still present an impasse, but within a few minutes the slopes ease and a simple descent can be made to the stream, and an obvious crossing point. At least two paths slant back up the opposite bank to join a contouring path in the bracken. Indeed, between these two climbing paths a short section of path traces the very course of the stream on its slabby bed.

Turn left up the other side on this level path, and while warning signs guard the old quarry site, a good path runs down through a brief rocky section to the floor of the old quarry. The main path rises outside the quarry confines, meeting the much used footpath descending from Great Hill via Drinkwaters. This slants down to a Ramblers' Association guidepost of 1963. Just below it the direct path swings sharp left beneath the grassy embankment of a former dam to arrive at a stone arched bridge over the Goit, to reach the cricket pitch at White Coppice. The Goit was built to carry water from the Roddlesworth reservoirs (see WALK 12) to Rivington.

If not desperate to finish, prolong the walk a little by turning sharp right at the path junction just yards below the guidepost, and follow the level path running the base of the moor above the Goit, with the upper reservoir across it. Reaching a sunken way at the forlorn ruin of Sharrocks, turn left down to cross a grassy, stone arched bridge on the Goit. Across, turn sharp left on a sometimes muddy path that emerges at the reedy head of the reservoir. The path then traces the grassy shoreline, and crosses the outflow to drop down to the cricket pitch. With luck, refreshments might be available here. **Turn right past the white-walled cottages and follow the rough road away. This leads to the road-end in White Coppice, continue on past the ford to the bridge and junction.**

White Coppice is a select, award-winning little hamlet tucked away from the outside world on a virtual cul-de-sac, with a delightful array of cottages and gardens. It is therefore difficult to imagine that, principally during the 19th century, the place was a hive of industrial activity. A number of factories and mills were scattered about the area we have just enjoyed, and to serve the workforce there would also have been far more houses than now exist. The abandoned industries thus explain the string of small dams occupying the valley, built to ensure the necessary water supply for powering the various works.

From the junction in the centre cross the bridge at Warth Farm and then go immediately left on a footbridge over the stream. Turn downstream on a thin path, quickly reaching the head of another reservoir. This is the first of the lower chain, and a super path runs along its western shore, fringed by trees. These also make a fine foreground to views back to Stronstrey Bank and the moor above. **At the end a stile returns us to the embankment between the reservoirs. Re-cross it and conclude back up through Causeway House Farm.**

3

ANGLEZARKE MOOR

START *Anglezarke*   *Grid ref. SD 621161*

DISTANCE *7¼ miles*

ORDNANCE SURVEY MAPS
1:50,000
Landranger 109 - Manchester
1:25,000
Explorer 19 - West Pennine Moors

ACCESS *Start from Leicester Mill Quarry car park on the eastern shore of Anglezarke Reservoir, above the dam. Bus service and rail station at Adlington, 2 miles off-route. There are some lay-bys nearer Alance Bridge on the walk's first half-mile. •ACCESS AREA - see page 8.*

Some rough walking over moorland best avoided after a prolonged wet spell. Lead Mines Clough is worth a visit whatever the weather, and enjoyment of this first stage may be enhanced by obtaining an inexpensive leaflet from local information centres.

S **From the car park drop back down to the road, and keep right to quickly reach a triangular junction. Go left on the Belmont road, rising a little before running outside the shore of Yarrow Reservoir. When the road turns to cross it at Alance Bridge, go straight ahead through a gate and along a cart track, with the arm of the reservoir still on the right. This runs on to bridge Limestone Brook at an access notice. Advance to a board imparting much information on the history of Lead Mines Clough, which we are now within. Just past it is a small waterfall, and a little further, another bridge.**

Lead mining operations here had a chequered history under various owners, and though last worked in 1837, there was little success other than for a spell in the 1780s. The site was excavated in the 1980s and revealed a surprising amount lost in a century and a half's under-growth. Invaluable work by the British Trust for Conservation Volunteers has resulted in a very worthwhile and absorbing little trail on a site that could easily have sunk into oblivion.

Leave the main track and cross the bridge to a kissing-gate to head upstream. Features of interest are a slime pit on the left and a sough on the right. The pit is a shallow hollow which retained particles of lead brought down in water used for washing the ore: the resulting lead-rich silt was then dug out. Across the stream is the small, dark hole of the sough, a level used for draining the workings. **Just further we reach the pumping shaft and waterwheel pit.** The wheel is likely to have been used to pump water from the shaft. **Behind it the public footpath is met just above a footbridge.** Two stone pillars ahead are launder bases, the supports of a wooden trough which brought water from a spring to serve the waterwheel.

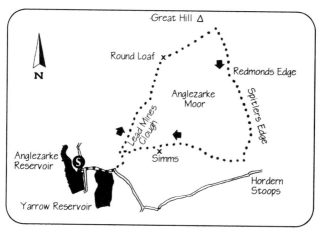

The footpath doubles back left up the bracken bank, meeting another path and doubling back again to a memorial cross at the top. A couple of seats invite a worthwhile pause, enjoying moorland views across to Winter Hill, Rivington Pike and the Pigeon Tower. The memorial pays tribute to the crew of six tragically killed when a Wellington bomber crashed on the moors above in November 1943. For a very short return, go left to the ladder-stile to quickly reach Jepson's Gate on the minor road above the car park.

A thin path continues along the bank from the memorial, forging upstream through bracken and foliage along the top edge of the clough. This grand stroll opens out with a view over the clough marred by the scattering of alien trees. A green path runs on to meet a broader one at a kissing-gate. Bear right along it with forestry on the left. This substantial plantation is not shown on the map revised in 1996! **On drawing level with a footbridge, detour across it to a stile to look down on a charming, heather-couched waterfall.**

The track runs upstream to a confluence, now truly on the open moor. A path takes over with the main (right) stream, and is followed for a few minutes before reaching a distinct fork. Take the left branch clambering up the bank, then running gently across the heather moor. Soon the unmistakeable landmark of the Round Loaf appears, backed by Great Hill. Sat like a pudding on the otherwise featureless Anglezarke Moor, it looks for all the world like a local version of Silbury Hill. **At a stream crossing the path turns to make a bee-line for the Loaf.** Its origins are uncertain, possibly being older than Bronze Age, perhaps dating back to Neolithic times - the New Stone Age. Certainly it was a type of burial mound, and is clearly a place of regular modern day pilgrimage. An inevitable cairn sits atop the dome, which measures roughly 50 yards across.

Of the innumerable trods radiating from the Loaf, take the most obvious one, which maintains the north-easterly direction of the approach path. Only very gently does it gain height, rather moistly crossing towards Dean Black Brook in front of the drier slopes of Great Hill. The way forks, though it matters little which is taken. On gaining the clough cross to find a thin path rising up the other side, quickly arriving at a watershed fence. Unless wishing to visit the top of Great Hill (see WALK 1), there is no need to cross the stile.

Our route is to the right, on the surprising discovery of a flagged path. This modern causey effects an easy crossing of the peaty watershed while preserving the fragile terrain. Flags from the floors of redundant mills are thus returned to the great outdoors in a fine example of recycling, following the fashion of many miles of the Pennine Way over the South Pennine moors. **The path winds unfailingly south across the broad moorland skyline.** Winter Hill stands directly ahead, while the view back to the left reveals Darwen Tower on its moortop. **An old wall is picked up and leads down to a pronounced saddle at Redmonds Edge before a pull onto Spitlers Edge.**

Advantage has been taken of this short, steep section to practice the technique of stone 'pitching', a style more commonly encountered on the Lakeland Fells. In 1997 this marked the limit of the stone causey. Views have by now opened out to the east, with Turton and Holcombe moors prominent, while down to the left Belmont's church spire and works chimney thrust out of the valley. **The old wall remains for company as the walk's highest point is reached at 1286ft/392m. A gentle decline then a level section precede arrival on a brow at Will Narr, overlooking the Belmont-Rivington road summit at Hordern Stoops.**

Descend the short steep section but then turn sharp right on a thin green path. This return path is a splendid stride in this upper section, working gently down to the ruins and trees at Higher Hempshaw's. The clough in front is that of the grandly named river Yarrow. **Here a broader track is met. Go right on it, over the tiny stream up to the lesser ruins of Lower Hempshaw's. Though the track goes right here, bear left between the low ruins and across the field alongside a crumbling wall. From the wall junction at the end (stile to the right) a moist path sets forth down the rough Sam Pasture. At the bottom a stream is crossed and the way rises improvingly to the ruins of Simms. A Peak & Northern Footpaths Society sign stands alongside.**

Go left to find a firm track running to a gate/ladder-stile. Head away on it, reaching some grassy mounds on the right. These are at the site of trial shafts from the mines, dug in the search for workable veins. **Just beyond, the track swings right to a good viewpoint overlooking the clough. Descend into it to rejoin the outward route, and return downstream to finish the walk as it began.**

*Waterfall,
Lead Mines Clough*

ANGLEZARKE RESERVOIR

START *Anglezarke* Grid ref. SD 621161

DISTANCE *4 miles*

ORDNANCE SURVEY MAPS
1:50,000
Landranger 109 - Manchester
1:25,000
Explorer 19 - West Pennine Moors

ACCESS *Start from Leicester Mill Quarry car park on the eastern shore of Anglezarke Reservoir, above the dam. Bus service and rail station at Adlington, 2 miles off-route.*

A straightforward reservoir circuit, with some splendid woodland and wide-ranging views.

❺ **Drop back down the drive to a kissing-gate on the right. A surfaced path heads north along the reservoir wallside through rich, colourful woodland.** A path from the upper car park signboard short-cuts its way down to join us. Leicester Mill Quarry is soon passed over to the right: the mill site is now below the reservoir. The extensive quarry provided stone for the reservoir, and untold kerbstones during its working life. Abandoned in the 1920s, its environs have been reclaimed by nature, and rock climbers have since found it an ideal playground. **The path heads round past an inlet, rising to a seat and birds information board. Here branch left on a better path to curve around the knoll, above the water. The path swings round high above the reservoir to drop to a crossroads of paths: go left.**

Our way escapes as a clear path into open country before running back to more woodland and a stile out onto Moor Road near the reservoir head. Go left past Heapey Waterman's Cottage. This is an attractive, isolated house built by Liverpool Corporation in the 1850s. Up to the right is a good prospect of the heathery, stony scarp of Stronstrey Bank (see WALK 2). **Crossing the reservoir head, leave immediately by a stile on the left to begin the return leg.**

A grand path runs above the shore through the fine woodland of Grey Heights Wood. The Waterman's Cottage is well seen backed by the moorland edge of Stronstrey Bank across the reedy reservoir head; there is also a good view down the length of the reservoir. **The path rises to a stile out of the wood, and a few yards across a field edge to a stile onto Heapey Fold Lane. Go left on this rough road.** Its broad grassy ridge affords grand views over the reservoir to the moorland above, with Rivington Pike and Winter Hill behind. To the right is a vast stretch of the plain beyond the M61 motorway.

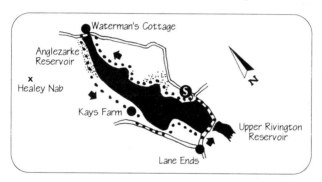

When the lane turns sharp right, keep straight on along the enclosed bridleway. Emerging onto a drive, go right to a back road, Charnock Back Lane. Turn left here past several dwellings, and soon after it narrows take a stile/gate on the left beneath the reservoir wall. Bear right to a stile and curve round to the left on a path beneath a lower wall. This soon swings left and rejoins the reservoir shore. The old quarries are now in view directly ahead.

A splendid final section leads round towards the dam, the latter part being deflected from the bank by walled woodland to a kissing-gate onto the road opposite a reservoir keeper's house. Go left along the embankment and keep left on the roadside footway. When it expires at a junction, go left a minute or two further to return to the car park entrance.

5

WINTER HILL
from Rivington

START *Rivington*   *Grid ref. SD 632144*

DISTANCE *6½ miles*

ORDNANCE SURVEY MAPS
1:50,000
Landranger 109 - Manchester
1:25,000
Explorer 19 - West Pennine Moors

ACCESS *Start from Rivington Hall Barn car park in the country park, off Rivington Lane between Rivington and Horwich. Buses at Horwich (with a seasonal service into the park). •ACCESS AREA - see page 8.*

An easy climb to the tops from Lever Park, best saved for a clear day.

S Winter Hill was the scene, in September 1896, of a monumental mass trespass that preceded the better known Kinder Scout event by several decades. Colonel Ainsworth of Smithills Hall (see WALK 7) closed the moorland paths to protect his grouse shooting interests, but the good folk of Bolton were outraged, and it is thought around 8000 people took part in the protest walk. They climbed the hill via Smithills Moor and descended to Belmont. A week later half as many again made the walk, though with less success as the Colonel had take legal action. Ultimately of course our rights were restored, and the event's centenary was celebrated by a walk over the route.

Dating from the 1780s, Rivington Hall boasts an attractive red brick frontage and much older origins. Rivington Hall Barn, alongside, was restored in the early 20th century, but its history is greater than the hall itself. Refreshments are sometimes available here.

From the car park, pass around the back of the barn and the hall to where the driveway ends at a lone house. Take a gateway to its right and a broad path heads off through the trees. Quickly emerging from enclosing fences it forks: bear right to remain on a level stroll through more open woodland. Early views up to the left feature the Pigeon Tower above the steep, wooded Terraced Gardens. This splendid stroll swings right to a crossroads in front of a lone house. Here turn left on the even broader, level way. Remain on this wide carriageway to its terminus on meeting a narrow, ascending road.

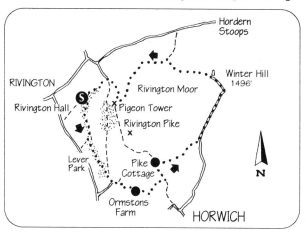

Go left, rising up the now concrete way. Through a gate, however, leave at the first opportunity by a gate/stile on the right. A charming green path contours along through open country. There are wide views over Horwich and the extensive plains beyond. Arriving at a deep wooded clough, the path quickly reaches a gate to access it. Don't advance on, but take a stile on the right to descend a wooden flight to a footbridge on the stream. This is a lovely spot: the stream itself is the infant river Douglas, fresh from its birth on the upper slopes of Winter Hill. The path climbs straight back out the other side to join a concrete access road.

Turn left up here, soon bearing away from the clough. Look back over part of Lower Rivington Reservoir and the adjacent motorway services. Ahead is the beckoning, sky-high mast, with Rivington Pike looking good across to the left. The drive runs on to Ormstons Farm,

25

continuing as a good track to a junction at the corner of Wilderswood. Here turn sharp left, climbing on a broad enclosed way outside the wood. This is left at the first chance by a branch left, which quickly swings back uphill to rise pleasantly through more open country. At the top it slants up a heather bank to the old road of Georges Lane.

Turn left on here for a few level minutes to Pike Cottage. This serves as a useful tearoom in this isolated spot. **A stile on its near side gives access to the open country of Winter Hill. A good path rises away, climbing enjoyably across the moor to eventually join the surfaced access road serving the summit installations. Before that, a chance to vary the route comes by taking a lesser path striking right, to gain the prominent massive cairn on the knoll of Crooked Edge Hill above. Constructed from a plentiful supply of outcropping stones, it has a nearby lesser partner, now joined by a third, amateur-built cairn. From here one could opt to either join the nearby road, or use a branch back to the main path.**

Either way, once the service road is joined it is but a simple, near level walk to the summit of the hill. New views to the south look over the moor to a vast sprawl of suburbia, though a clear day will reveal the South Pennines running along to merge into the northern heights of the Peak District. Near the road are some of the many small coal pits that were worked on the hill a couple of centuries ago. **The road runs past the first buildings, huddled beneath the massive TV mast, and the adjacent Scotsman's Stump.**

A tablet on the building recalls the Winter Hill air disaster of February 1958, just one of a number of aircraft crashes this hill has witnessed. The 'stump' is a more personal, iron monument, recording the tragic end met by one George Henderson, a pedlar from Dumfries-shire shot while crossing the moor in November 1838. Though there may be less likelihood of being shot today, a modern winter danger is that of ice detaching itself from the mast and its supports: a blade of ice falling several hundred feet is more than enough to achieve a tragic end!

Keep on to a sharp bend and bear left on the service road past various installations. The Ordnance Survey column stands to the right. A rougher option is to take the stile in front and follow the 'wild' side of the fence to a stile giving access to the OS column. This poor, bewildered trig. point, so often a lone hilltop sentinel, looks more than a little lost in this eerie land of the giants!

At 1496ft/456m this is the highest point on the West Pennine Moors and despite the distractions, it gives the most extensive, if not the most impressive, of views. The girth of its broad top results in eyes straining to pick out distant features, assuming visibility permits! Apart from the overpowering 1000ft/300m TV mast, Telecom and Police masts are among the sundry supporting cast. To be fair, the distant view really is something on a clear day, reaching far beyond the West Pennine scene to the mountains of Snowdonia, the Lake District and the Yorkshire Dales. Additionally there is a long Pennine skyline to the east, running as far down as Kinder Scout in the Peak District, and a number of man-made objects such as Blackpool Tower on the Lancashire coast. Middle distance hill country includes Bowland and Pendle to the north, while in front of the North Wales' peaks is the Clwydian Range of hills and moors.

Winter Hill from the cairn on Noon Hill

After the last installation, keep on the left side of the fence. This quickly drops steeply down the northern face (see WALK 8), but simply remain on the clear path running west along the very well defined edge. Rivington Tower appears ahead, and there are grand views north over moors, and west to the reservoirs, the plain, and possibly the coast. **A splendid few minutes are enjoyed on this dry path, which all too soon drops sharply down the declining edge to a stile onto Lord Leverhulme's Belmont Road.**

Note that it is possible to stay on high ground longer by continuing due west on a fading path, down through a marshy patch to the distinct knoll of Noon Hill out on the end. Its cairn sits on the very pronounced mound of a Bronze Age burial cairn, possibly 3000 years old. From there a thin trod resumes west, dropping steeply to a stile onto the old road. The plantation below the road has not yet made it onto the map.

On the old road, meanwhile, turn left for a largely level stroll around the base of Noon Hill. The rough road runs round to arrive at a junction at the landmark of the Pigeon Tower. This elaborate dovecote dates from 1910, and is a legacy of the enthusiasm of Lord Leverhulme when he created the wonders of the gardens on the slopes below. Restored in the 1970s, its position is outstanding, and as a viewpoint alone it is the popular objective of many a family walk. Rivington Pike, with its own, less inspiring tower, is a tempting few minutes south along the old road.

Here is a choice of routes. To sample the Terraced Gardens, turn to WALK 6, which descends to the Hall Barn through them. Otherwise, double back sharp right on the similarly rough road which runs down, more steeply in its lower part to arrive at the Lower House car park. Level with the car park take a ladder-stile on the left, and cross to a stile into a corner of fenced woodland. The path runs on the fence side to quickly leave the wood, joining a cart track just in front. Turn left on this a few yards to a junction, and here turn right to descend outside the wooded clough. This same track leads directly down to quickly return to the start.

The Pigeon Tower

6

RIVINGTON PIKE

START *Rivington*   *Grid ref. SD 628138*

DISTANCE *4½ miles*

ORDNANCE SURVEY MAPS
1:50,000
Landranger 109 - Manchester
1:25,000
Explorer 19 - West Pennine Moors

ACCESS *Start from Great House Barn Visitor Centre, on Rivington Lane just south of Rivington. Nearest buses are at Horwich, to the south, with summer services into Lever Park itself.*

A stiff pull to a celebrated viewpoint, with much else of interest in this exploration of a superb country park. An extremely useful purchase from the information centre is a leaflet describing the many features of the Terraced Gardens. The colours in autumn are quite memorable.

❺ Rivington is the old estate of the de Rivingtons, which after several changes of ownership was purchased in 1900 by William Hesketh Lever. This highly successful businessman was best known for his soap 'empire' based at Port Sunlight. Later to become Lord Leverhulme, he created the delights of Lever Park and the Terraced Gardens before his death. As early as 1902 he gifted the park to the people of Bolton.

Great House Barn is a magnificent, restored cruck framed barn of great age (illustrated on page 1). It now operates as a West Pennine Moors Countryside Service information centre and a welcome and popular cafe. **From the visitor centre cross to the bottom end of the car park and pass a play area to follow a path towards the reservoir. At a fence outside its environs turn left, the path crossing a footbridge and running on to merge into a broader one. Simply remain on this with**

woodland on the right and the open park on the left. Lovely views look across the park to the Pigeon Tower and Rivington Pike on the skyline, both above the steep wooded slopes of the Terraced Gardens. The big mast on Winter Hill rises between the towers. **The path soon reaches the ruin of Liverpool Castle in the trees.** Completed (if that's the correct word for a purpose built ruin!) by Lord Leverhulme in 1925, it is a replica of Liverpool Castle as it stood at the end of the Civil War. It affords a good view over the reservoir.

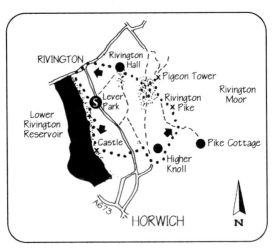

Leave by the main path heading away into the park at an angle from the castle, and remain on this broad avenue to approach the Middle Derbyshires car park on the right. At this point bear left on a thinner but clear path to join Rivington Lane. Cross straight over and up an enclosed bridleway. This almost loses itself on opening out into the woodland above, but continue straight up to join the carriageway of a broad, rough road. Turn right to meet a narrow, ascending road.

Go left, rising up the now concrete way. When it turns left for the farm of Higher Knoll, keep straight on up the lesser path to a gate. This continues to climb steeply but pleasantly, with the tower looming above. On meeting the contouring old road of Georges Lane, cross straight over and resume uphill on another rough road. As it swings right to outflank the highest point, a path breaks off for a direct assault on the upper slopes to gain the top of Rivington Pike.

Sat proudly on the top is Rivington Tower, a popular landmark and objective of many thousands of walks each year from the park below - as the essential restoration of our descent path testifies. It was built in 1733 by John Andrews, then owner of the Rivington Manor estate. A mere 20ft high, it stands 1187ft/362m above sea level. The room inside, where shooting parties once took shelter, is now rendered inaccessible on safety grounds. As recently as 1967 the tower was almost demolished by Liverpool Corporation, but was saved by public outcry and survives today as a listed building. The Pike was part of the same gift to the public as the park, far below, in 1902. Long before the tower appeared, this knoll was a beacon site, one of a vast chain throughout the country on which fires were lit to warn of impending danger (such as the approach of the Spanish Armada in 1588) or more recently to celebrate important, often Royal events.

Rivington Pike's greatest appeal is as a viewpoint, for being sited on the edge of Winter Hill yet sufficiently detached, it earns sweeping views over the plains while retaining its links with the nearby moors. On gaining the top, Winter Hill's thousand foot TV mast is joined by its supporting cast, while just along the old road to our north is the more engaging Pigeon Tower. A clear day reveals a fascinating array of features to the west. Here the mountain skylines of Snowdonia and the Lake District might be on offer. Nearer but still many miles distant are Helsby Hill and across the Welsh border, the hills of the Clwydian Range; Blackpool Tower is an inevitable object to be sought out by many; while further north the rolling moors of Bowland are on show.

Descend the stone staircase from the tower, meeting the first rough road to then run along to join the main one. On the left is a toilet block at an alternative entrance to the Terraced Gardens. **The best route walks the five minutes along the old road to the beckoning Pigeon Tower.** This elaborate dovecote dates from 1910, and is a legacy of the enthusiasm of Lord Leverhulme when he created the wonders of the gardens on the slopes below. Restored in the 1970s, its position is quite outstanding (illustrated on page 28). **Just before the Pigeon Tower, a concession bridleway doubles back left, down into the Terraced Gardens.** This is where the leaflet pays for itself, identifying a bewildering number of features (some numbers are mentioned in the description overleaf). Our route through the gardens takes in a fair section of the leaflet route, albeit in reverse. Alternatively, ignore the whole of the ensuing instructions and just find your own way - it's probably more fun anyway!

These quite extraordinary grounds were laid out during the first quarter of the 20th century by Lever. Improvements were still being made when he died in 1925. Sadly the gardens became derelict, and most of Lever's dream was lost beneath many years of undergrowth. After a spell in the hands of a Bolton brewer, the estate was then acquired by Liverpool Corporation to extend their water gathering grounds. North West Water took over responsibility on its formation in 1974, not too late to begin the long process of restoration. For what we see today, a great debt of gratitude is owed to the sterling work of the British Trust for Conservation Volunteers.

The path first runs on to the site of a bungalow and ballroom, some small sections of tiled floor remaining in this open area. At the far end, the main path forks. Take neither but turn down steps (22) on the right, slanting left at a fork to reach a junction above an elaborate balcony overlooking the former Great Lawn.

Beneath the balcony with its pillars and shelter, turn left on the 'crazy paving' path. At a T-junction turn right down a stepped path under a stone archway, to a junction with a broader path. Cross straight over and down a narrow path past the base of a stone house (17), then bear left to arrive at one side or the other of the ornamental lake in the Japanese Garden. From the far end (9), double back a few yards on the path NOT by its shore, and another branch drops away onto Roynton Lane.

A gate on the left provides escape from the gardens. Ignore this and cross straight over, down a zigzag path. After the first bend ignore the following zigzags, and keep straight on the contouring path. This runs on to a stream crossing, with stone cave shelters just across. Turn down the near side of the stream, a stepped path descending to swing right over a stone arched bridge in the environs of the Ravine. This fair scene successfully belies the hand of man in enhancing nature's own good work.

From here remain on the Terrace path, a grand walk which leads on above the substantial remains of the stone built Garden Shelter to a fork. Here take the broader way slanting down to the left, dropping down to the bottom corner of the wood. Emerging, the track descends the fieldside to a gate/stile into woods, and another crossroads of ways. Continue straight down, merging with another path and bearing right to quickly arrive at the rear of Rivington Hall.

Past the lone house, follow the drive along the rear of the buildings to emerge alongside Rivington Hall Barn. Dating from the 1780s, Rivington Hall boasts an attractive red brick frontage and much older origins. Rivington Hall Barn, alongside, was restored in the early 20th century, but its history is greater than the hall itself. Refreshments are often available here.

Cross the car park and where the surfaced drive and a much broader, rough road fork, bear right on the latter. Part way along, look out for a clear footpath branching off right. This runs along the field edge to the far corner. Before leaving, take a look back to the Pigeon Tower and woods, with Rivington Tower also appearing. **A kissing-gate leads onto Sheep House Lane alongside Chapel House. Turn left, down to the green and junction.** Just prior to the junction is a popular refreshments outlet. Alongside is Rivington Unitarian Chapel, with its datestone of 1703: this was Lancashire's first non-conformist place of worship. Some attractive cottages and the village stocks also feature.

Continue straight down the road, now with a footway. The church stands hidden up to the right: part dating from its rebuilding of 1540. On the left is Rivington school, dating from 1714 and founded in 1566 as a grammar school. **Turn left on a short driveway past the school. Beyond a small parking area the broad path splits. Bear left into the more open country of the park, and then almost at once branch right on a thinner footpath, still very clear. This runs a splendid course alongside scattered woodland to quickly return to the start.**

Liverpool Castle

33

7

SMITHILLS DEAN

START *Barrow Bridge*   *Grid ref. SD 687117*

DISTANCE *6 miles*

ORDNANCE SURVEY MAPS
1:50,000
Landranger 109 - Manchester
1:25,000
Explorer 19 - West Pennine Moors

ACCESS *Start from Barrow Bridge car park. It is reached from the A58 north-west of Bolton, either by way of Smithills Dean Road (Smithills Hall signs), left on Smithills Croft Road, then right at the big chimney; or Moss Lane past Moss Bank Park, and past the chimney. The road passes toilets/bus turning circle, then narrows to lead through the old village to the large car park. Bus from Bolton to the turning circle. Smithills Hall makes a good alternative start, with a direct bus service.*

An easy and very enjoyable circuit of Smithills Dean, an unassuming side valley on the flanks of Winter Hill and yet also on the edge, almost, of Bolton (though you wouldn't know it). Striking, naturally wooded cloughs add much colour at regular intervals, while Smithills Hall makes a contrastingly cultural diversion. The autumn colours can be quite outstanding, with or without sunshine.

⑤ Barrow Bridge sprung up as a village in 1846, housing workers for its two spinning mills. Their closure, however, led to a demise that left the place known as the 'Deserted Village'. Surviving cottages have happily been restored and Barrow Bridge is now designated a conservation area, with its own history trail. Most of the old village is passed en route to the start point. **From the car park turn left up the narrow road, past attractive houses accessed by bridges on the stream.** These originally housed the mill 'management'. **At the sharp**

bend don't cross the bridge, but advance straight on the streamside to a high flight of steps. This sturdy stone staircase was built over two centuries ago for colliers and quarrymen to reach their moorland employment. **Climb the ridge-end steps above the confluence.** On the left is the engaging Dakin's Brook, and the main stream, Dean Brook (High Shore's Clough) is on the right.

At the top the path runs on to a kissing-gate, then continues along the grassy ridge. Ahead, the slopes of Smithills Moor rise towards Winter Hill with its ubiquitous monster mast pointing to the skies. **Quickly forking, the left branch leaves the fence to cross to the far corner of the pasture and the head of the wooded clough of Dakin's Brook, a now insignificant stream. A stile gives access to a streamside path which runs a pleasant, enclosed course up onto Walker Fold Road.**

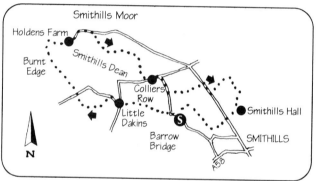

Virtually opposite, a narrow road climbs away past the houses at Little Dakins Farm. Approaching a bend several paths leave the road. Take the first stile on the left and head away with the crumbling wall. At the end a footbridge admits to the semi-rough pasture of Fleet's Moor. Slant directly up the centre of this pasture to an old field boundary where five paths converge - though there's little evidence! Now head straight up the centre with the line of another old boundary, through reeds to a stile at the top.

The extensive views exhibit a typical West Pennines contrast of open country and a vast, not so distant sprawl of urban town and cityscape. **Head diagonally away again, up the centre to a stile at the far corner. Here bear right along the fieldside, continuing along the mound of an old boundary to rise onto a rough back road, Matchmoor Lane.**

Cross straight over and up the inviting green way heading away. When this crosses the brow and fades, keep straight on with the crumbling wall, maintaining this line alongside increasingly moor-like terrain. At the sturdier wall corner take a stile in the ensuing fence, and a path runs on through a new pocket of native woodland to a kissing-gate onto a junction of ways. In front are the heather colonised remains of an old quarry.

From the gate on the right a cart track around the rim of Burnt Edge is joined. This is a grand spot to break journey, amid patches of heather on a steep bank overlooking the upper reaches of Smithills Dean. Down in the bottom is the site of Burnt Edge Colliery, one of many coal mining sites on Winter Hill's extensive flanks. Go left on the track, accompanied by a larger heather tract on the left. The track runs on to a junction just short of Dean Brook in Holden's Plantation. The main track (not our route) swings left to climb onto Smithills Moor. The access area is now very close at this point, offering the opportunity to join the masts' service road for a quick ascent of Winter Hill.

Advance a little further to the ruins and new plantings which will in time further enhance the very edge of the clough. Now double sharply back down to the right, on the near side of the steep bank. A rough track re-forms and bridges the clough. On leaving, head away with an old wall on the right, and a rough lane is soon entered to lead on to Holdens Farm just ahead.

The route runs on through the farm and out along the access road. The farmyard can be avoided by an enclosed bridle-path on the right, skirting round the front to join the drive at the far gate. Head away on the road until reaching a second wooded clough. On the left are a stile and access notice, and it is worth two or three minutes up the clough-side path to savour its colour and character. More extensive areas of new tree plantings are in evidence. The route turns down the drive on the right, in tandem with the clough to reach a former farm.

Though the path strictly passes left of all the buildings, an unstable barn renders it necessary to drop down left between the two lower barns to emerge back above the clough. This situation may change slightly at some future point. The path runs down above the clough before quickly descending into it. Enjoy just a brief flirtation with its grandeur before climbing back up the other side. Pause to look back down at the lively little waterslides on the stream.

From a stile head away to the house at Sheep Cote Green Farm and follow its drive out. Crossing yet another wooded clough and passing Chadwick's Close Farm, the rough road rises to a fork. Here turn right, descending between Hampsons Farm buildings and past the heather colonised Brown Stones Quarry. There are good views to the right back over the route. The lane drops down onto a very broad road at Old Colliers Row. Perhaps not surprisingly, this appealing stone terrace housed the colliers from the nearby coalpits.

Smithills Hall

Turn left on the footway to a road junction at New Colliers Row. This too lives up to its name, and alongside, bearing a datestone of 1885, is the former school their children attended. Turn down the contrastingly narrower Longshaw Ford Road. Tempting paths accompany the adjacent tree-lined stream. At a junction with a farm road, there is the chance to be finished within five minutes by simply continuing straight down. Otherwise, turn left on the drive to Pendlebury's Farm, and bearing round to the right of the buildings the path runs on at the head of another wooded clough. Down to the right is the preserved Barrow Bridge chimney, often visible during the walk.

The enclosed bridlepath runs on to emerge onto the very broad Smithill Dean Road. Turn down the footway, and leave at the first chance by a drive on the left. Passing an imposing house of 1842 at Dean Gate Farm, it winds on to approach Tippett House. As the drive swings up to the house, turn right on a green track down the field centre to enter the woods.

Take the path bearing left, dropping past an abandoned lodge house and then tracing the outside of a high wall. Over to the left is a lively stream. At the end of the wall turn right along the front of what is currently a derelict site. Follow the drive out to a junction at the rear of Smithills Coaching House, and turn left to it. Here a restaurant operates in the preserved coach house and stables. **In front a gate admits to woodland, with Smithills Hall just ahead. A path heads away to cross a bridge with a nice little waterfall below. Across, bear left at the rear of Smithills Hall to emerge into the lovely grounds.**

Smithills Hall is an extensive and splendid house dating back to the 14th century. Surviving from the original fortified manor house is the Great Hall, though the east wing dates from Henry VIII's time. Numerous ensuing periods are represented, with the Victorian extensions dominant. Built by William de Ratcliffe, the house later passed to the Ainsworth family, a locally infamous member being the Colonel Ainsworth who strived to keep the public off his moorland slopes on Winter Hill. In 1938 Bolton Corporation acquired the house, part of which is open to the public as a museum. A countryside warden service was established in 1994, and efforts are being made to restore more of the house and gardens.

Also freely available to explore are the lovely grounds surrounding the house. A nature trail can be followed through the woodlands, and altogether there is much to see. Extending north of the house - and largely occupying the area of the walk - are the 2000 acres of the Smithills estate. Remarkably its boundary remains little changed from so many centuries ago, and still includes the same parkland, woodland, farmland and moorland.

Leave by the drive from the other side of the hall, running out to Smithills Dean Road. Cross straight over and along a snicket, which after interruption by a suburban road runs on between gardens to emerge onto the edge of a wooded clough. Don't take the main path straight on, but turn immediately right past the fences of the last few houses. Stile and gate admit into a field. Rise up the centre to a gate at the top, and continue up a rough track to Sheep House Farm above (a riding school). Ahead, the Winter Hill mast makes its final appearance. **Left of the buildings a stile admits onto an enclosed track. Turn left on this short-lived way, and from a stile an enclosed pathway runs on the fieldsides, dropping to a sloping bridge conveniently depositing us exactly at the start point.**

8

WINTER HILL
from Belmont

START *Belmont*   *Grid ref. SD 674158*

DISTANCE *5½ miles*

ORDNANCE SURVEY MAPS
1:50,000
Landranger 109 - Manchester
1:25,000
Explorer 19 - West Pennine Moors

ACCESS *Start from Hordern Butts Delf car park, on Rivington Road a half-mile west of the village. Belmont is served by bus from Bolton, and from Blackburn via Tockholes (the walk passes through the village centre). •ACCESS AREA - see page 8.*

A short but invigorating ascent of the area's major hill, whose steep slopes dominate the village of Belmont.

❺ From the car park use steps down to a path downstream to the head of Ward's Reservoir, better known locally as the Blue Lagoon. Paths on either bank lead to the dam, where the road is joined to enter the village, past the church to the junction at the *Black Dog* pub. Belmont is best known for the TV mast atop Winter Hill, many no doubt recall hearing its name in reference to the said installation. For a small settlement it retains a major employer in its dyeing and bleaching company. The centrally placed *Black Dog* dates from the mid-18th century, a popular pub serving outstanding and good value ales from the independent Manchester brewers, Holts. Surprisingly the village supports two other pubs, the *Black Bull* and the *Wrights Arms*. St. Peter's church is a resplendent building seeming out of scale to such a small community. There is also a Post office/store.

At the road junction outside the *Black Dog* a fountain, now decorated with flowers, recalls Queen Victoria's Diamond Jubilee of 1897. **Cross the main road and turn down the side road at Maria Square.** Plaques on the corner house identify both the name and the date 1804. **Pass the attractive cottages and descend the traffic-free lower section past a millpond to join Egerton Road alongside the dyeworks.**

Go left past the works and away gently up the road. Levelling off, look for an enclosed green way coming down on the left. Just 20 yards beyond it, step into the field on the right and descend to the bottom. Here a long footbridge crosses the outflow of the Ornamental Reservoir. This circuitous approach to Winter Hill affords a good opportunity to appraise it properly before setting foot on it. The hill is well seen across the reservoir, as are the works chimney and church steeple.

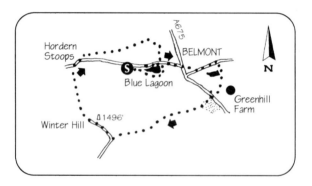

Across the dam the path forks. Go right to the stile in front, by the old sluice gate. Climb the bank into the field. A thin path rises above the deep wooded clough. **At the top corner go right with the garden fence of Greenhill Farm, and at the end keep on above the reedy stream head, doubling back towards the *Wrights Arms*.** The path joins the main road via the pub car park. **Go left 75 yards and take a gate into the corner of a plantation.** A broad path heads away, rising to enter the access area at a kissing-gate onto an old driveway.

Cross straight over and up the broad path slanting away. This same path rises without complication all the way to the summit of Winter Hill. The first stage is a well engineered section, built to serve old coal mines on the hill: a sunken way parallels the lower section. As height is gained Belmont Reservoir appears behind the village, and an ever increasing sweep of moorland is revealed. A fenced mineshaft is passed on the right, and later the way eases up to run past the site of a mine level in the mounds on the right just before the top. Two centuries ago, numerous small scale collieries operated on the flanks of Winter Hill.

Either cross the stile in the watershed fence, advance past a memorial cairn to join the service road and follow it right to gain the Ordnance Survey column; or stay on the near side of the fence and follow it right to a stile giving access to the same objective. Either way, it is difficult not to be distracted by the mass of human interference. The poor, bewildered trig. point, so often a lone hilltop sentinel, looks more than a little lost in this eerie land of the giants! For more on Winter Hill, please see WALK 5.

Resume beyond the trig. point, either by road or back to the fence. If still on the road, it must be vacated when it ends at the last installation, crossing to a fence-stile. Just yards further the ground falls away steeply. Descend the fence-side path with care before crossing the marshy shelf of Winter Hill Flats in company with the fence. This makes quite a contrast after the pampered ascent route. **At the end, the top of the Belmont-Rivington road at Hordern Stoops suddenly appears, surprisingly just a couple of minutes below.** A boundary stone has been incorporated into a restored section of wall, though all that can be read is the word *boundary!* Here the access area is left behind.

Turn right for a short while towards Belmont, quickly leaving by a stile on the left. Winter Hill's masts reach skyward up to the right, while ahead Belmont's church spire returns. **A smashing path contours away, and with only an occasional moist moment enjoys a splendid stride around the hillside. It passes a former quarry at Hoar Stones Brow, on through an old wall and slants down to meet a stile in the wall below. Head away with the fence to a stile at the end.**

For the Blue Lagoon, turn right down the fieldside concession path to emerge onto the road by the reservoir foot. For the village centre, advance straight on, forking right to reach a suburban street end. Here go right, down a snicket, then left on Ryecroft Lane out past the school onto the main road. The start is two minutes to the right.

LONGWORTH CLOUGH

9

START *Belmont*   *Grid ref. SD 674158*

DISTANCE *6 miles*

ORDNANCE SURVEY MAPS
1:50,000
Landranger 109 - Manchester
1:25,000
Explorer 19 - West Pennine Moors

ACCESS *Start from the central junction outside the Black Dog pub, by the church. Roadside parking. Served by bus from Bolton, and from Blackburn via Tockholes. Another useful start, mid-route, is from the King William IV pub at Dimple on the A666 (Blackburn-Bolton bus).*

An attractive wooded clough in the first half of the walk is complemented by a rougher moorland return, with the hamlet of Dimple midway, offering refreshments and a slice of history.

S For a note on Belmont, please see page 39. **From the *Black Dog* junction cross the main road and turn down the side road at Maria Square.** Plaques on the corner house identify both the name and the date 1804. **Pass the attractive cottages and descend the traffic-free lower section past a millpond to join Egerton Road alongside the dyeworks.** This offers its own particular smells. **Go left past the works and away gently up the road. Levelling off, look for an enclosed green way coming down on the left. Just 20 yards beyond it, step into the field on the right and descend to the bottom. Here a long footbridge crosses the outflow of the Ornamental Reservoir.**

Across the dam the path forks. Don't take the stile in front but turn left on a path which shadows the old mill-race. This still carries a flow of water: also, look back through the trees to the left to see a

42

substantial weir beneath the dam. **The path traces the leat for a considerable time, initially through woodland of the steeper clough and then more open country.** Longworth Clough is now outspread, with the moorland slopes of Winter Hill rising to the right. **The cut fades as the group of buildings at Low Fold appears ahead. Advance towards them, joining the drive but not entering the yard.** The main house is a fine building seeing recent renovation work.

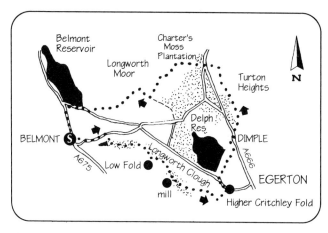

Without entering the yard, turn down the fieldside on the left, arriving above the steep wooded bank of the clough. The path winds down to meet Eagley Brook, which is followed pleasantly downstream. Much of the clough is designated a nature reserve, largely on account of the flowers that flourish here. There is also a strong likelihood of startling a heron. **After this last section the path climbs gently away, and runs on through scrubby terrain to suddenly reach the edge of the large industrial works that has been in view a while.** This busy concern is a huge paper mill covering a vast area.

The paper mill is reached alongside an old dam. Advance a few yards on the rough track, and with relief escape left on a stepped path dropping back down into the trees (not as per map). The path then shadows the stream again through this woodland, and on emerging into more open country merges into a path descending from the works. Just ahead a footbridge carries the path to the other bank to resume downstream, initially through a large heath-like pasture.

At the end the path runs on as a broader track to a stone arched bridge on the brook. Don't cross, but rise left on the grassy track for just 60 yards to find a little path climbing to a stile on the left. Head up the fieldside to another stile, and on again to a gate and gap-stile at Higher Critchley Fold. A short walled green way leads out onto Longworth Road alongside. To the right is the suburbia of Egerton.

Go left for a short while and leave by a footpath on the right, beneath the grassy embankment of Delph Reservoir. This runs an enclosed course to cross the outflow, then rising between castellated water board walls to arrive at Walmsley Chapel. This attractive corner features Walmsley Unitarian Chapel, founded before 1632, and built in 1712, in its graveyard and with the school of 1851 alongside. Don't follow the beech-lined avenue out to the road, but keep left up through a gate/gap-stile, and a thin path runs up the fieldside to arrive at the cluster of houses at Dimple. Just yards to the right on the A666 Blackburn-Bolton road stands the *King William IV* pub. The main road can partly be avoided by turning left on the briefly cobbled street between the houses. This is the former Blackburn-Bolton turnpike of 1796, crossed by the modern road at the pub and continuing north on a parallel course to the west.

When this rough road swings left through a gate, turn right on an enclosed green way which runs back to the main road. Cross to the footway and turn left, briefly. Take a stile on the right in front of a pocket plantation, and head away past it and up the wallside to the top of another plantation. Advance just a little further to a gate in a fence, and go left across the small enclosure. Ignore a step-stile on the right, and continue directly away along the base of Turton Heights. The fence on the right is followed to the far end, largely on a neat little 'ridge'. Delph Reservoir is well seen down to the left beyond the plantation and the road.

At the end a plantation corner is reached. The path shown as passing through the trees is non-existent, so use the gate and head away on the rough moor edge alongside the plantation. The trees quickly end, and a stile transfers us back to the reedy pasture. Continue on, contouring across with the main road below. Aim to reach a small cluster of trees at an old ruin: surmounting the knoll in front to the fence corner, an old sunken way drops back down to this point. Head away on another sunken way which slants gently right, rising imperceptibly across the pasture. This runs an infallible course, curving on to meet a junction of such ways in front of an attractive reedy pool. Turn left down the old way which runs straight as an arrow to the main road. A stile just to the left gives access. Cross with extreme care to a junction with a side road, and go straight ahead at the stile/gate into the trees of Charter's Moss Plantation.

A good track runs on to quickly emerge onto grassy moorland. Remain on the track past a reedy pool, and just short of a cluster of trees, a second waymark encountered sends a thin path down into Owshaw Clough, passing above a gushing water outflow. Across, the path goes right a few yards then slants up onto the level moor. Heading away, the thin path soon forks and becomes less clear. The aim is to reach a firm track directly ahead, climbing onto Longworth Moor. The corner of Stones Bank Plantation over to the left is a useful guide, for the track will be joined not far to its right. Forge on, avoid the worst of some intervening moister moments, and with luck a low ruin will be reached. From this a broadening green track heads away, crossing a couple of small side-streams to a gate in a fence. The track runs on to another gate to join the unmissable main track.

Turn right through the gate, and follow the gently rising track for about 150 yards. When it bends right, continue just a few yards with it to the Peak & Northern Footpaths Society guidepost marking a path junction. Here leave the track and turn left as directed for Belmont, a faint way running on alongside a minor drain. Directly ahead is the top edge of a young plantation with Winter Hill, as ever, rising behind. The plantation is not shown on the current map, 'revised' in 1996. The path becomes clearer as it crosses a stile in an old wall, and crosses a deep intervening clough to reach the far plantation corner. The moor is vacated here, and the way runs along a wallside with the farm at Higher Whittaker down to the left.

At the end, above the farm, advance on through the centre of the pasture. Belmont reveals itself just ahead, with Belmont Reservoir to the right. Towards the end slant down to the left of the trees ahead, to find a stile onto the back road. Go right, meeting the corner of Belmont Reservoir and crossing the embankment. Completed in 1826, the reservoir presents a colourful scene when the sailing club is in full swing: its moorland backdrop presents a more permanent scene. At the end short-cut the road by a little path slanting left up onto the main road on the edge of the village. Turn left on the footway to walk the greater length of the village to return to the start.

TURTON MOOR

START *Belmont*   *Grid ref. SD 665191*

DISTANCE *5½ miles*

ORDNANCE SURVEY MAPS
1:50,000
Landranger 109 - Manchester
1:25,000
Explorer 19 - West Pennine Moors

ACCESS *Start from Crookfield Road car park just off the A675 Preston-Bolton road, fully 2 miles north of Belmont. Served by Blackburn-Belmont buses, and Sunday Blackburn-Bolton via Belmont buses.*

A grand moorland stride encircling Turton Moor on a fine range of paths and tracks.

S **From the car park pass through the picnic area to join the road at a sharp bend. Cross and take the firm cart track heading away.** This is the old Bolton to Preston coach road: we shall travel an extended section of it to conclude the walk. **With a crumbling wall on the left, leave at the first opportunity through an old gateway. A green track now resembling a drain slants up the field towards the ruin of Higher Pasture Barn Farm. From a stile to its left a Landrover track slants up above the small clough.**

When the track swings sharp left remain on the path, soon crossing the stream and rising to a gateway in an old wall on the brow. This is a splendid place to halt, looking ahead to Holcombe Moor, the Peel Tower and much Pennine moorland beyond. Behind us, the ground falls away steeply before rising to Winter Hill and Great Hill. This spot is marked by a well-sited seat and a weathered Peak District & Northern Counties Footpath Preservation Society guidepost, 1960 vintage (see page 3). Now the less cumbersome Peak & Northern Footpaths Society, this venerable organisation celebrated its centenary in 1994, and though its attractive guideposts proliferate in the Peak District, it's nice to see them pointing the way in this region also.

Head away on the broad path, commencing a long, gentle descent between Darwen and Turton Moors: ignore an early branch left at a cairn. Passing an old shaft the path runs down, soon in the company of a neatly culverted, swift-flowing stream. The splendid path passes through a stile and winds down to swing sharply to cross a similarly enclosed sidestream, now in the head of the Cadshaw Valley. This once thriving dale was rendered lifeless after Liverpool Corporation acquired the area for water catchment. On the skyline to the right are the landmarks of the Big Grey Stones on Turton Moor.

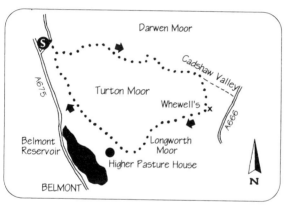

A little further, the scant remains of a farm are reached just before the first tree. Here leave the green track and descend a slimmer path to a small footbridge on the stream. The path rises away past former workings to join a level green trackway. This would have served one of the moor's old collieries. **Go left, enjoying more grand strides as it gently declines off the moor.** Ahead, the distinct knoll of Hog Lowe Pike is seen to the left of the unbroken Holcombe Moor skyline.

Though our green track can be seen running straight as a die down onto the A666 Blackburn-Bolton road, it is left long before then at a crossroads with a very faint path. Happily this is marked by another PNFS guidepost. Here strike off right, traces of an embanked track

lead along the green pasture to a lone tree at the ruins of Whewell's. A former occupant was George Whewell, who during the Civil War is said to have performed the execution of the Earl of Derby at Bolton.

Continue on past the ruin on a distinct course to a stile back onto rough moorland. A thin path heads away, running a delectable course around the flanks of Turton Moor, maintaining a most efficient contour. Entwistle Reservoir is well seen down to the left, enclosed by dark plantations. Further, the gaunt prospect of Winter Hill returns impressively ahead. **Traces of a descending wall are crossed and the very scant remains of a building.** A handful of old roof slates are neatly stacked up. **Just a little further the path meets a clearer one slanting up from the plantation down to the left. Bear right on this to quickly reach the substantial ruins of a farm.** Here several old buildings are in evidence, making this as good a place as any for a lunch break.

Leave by slanting gently left, crossing a streamlet and an old wall and ideally locating the faint path that runs across to meet a well defined, unmistakeable green track. This is the bed of a former tramway leading down from the mine. Just above, the old spoil heaps are still in evidence, but before reaching them branch left on another thin path. Crossing two small streams (one with an old wall in front; the second just below a confluence) rise slightly right to find the minor ruin of Moor Side Farm.

The invisible footpath contours south-west over Longworth Moor to reach the old coach road, but an easy (and useful!) mistake is to follow a broad green track leaving the ruin, which slants south-south-west down the moor to meet the old road a little further south. Turn right on the old road, still a very serviceable cart track, the point of merging with the true footpath being marked by another PNFS guidepost.

From that point onward the track runs an undulating course along the moorside, passing above the farm at Higher Pasture House. Belmont Reservoir makes a fine foreground to Belmont village nestling beneath the steep slopes of Winter Hill, the tall church spire being especially upstanding. Completed in 1826, the reservoir presents a particularly colourful scene when the sailing club is in full swing. **The track runs unfailingly on past Lower Pasture Barn Farm, keeping straight on to pick up the outward route just short of the start.**

11

DARWEN TOWER

START *Darwen*   *Grid ref. SD 679224*

DISTANCE *4¾ miles*

ORDNANCE SURVEY MAPS
1:50,000
Landranger 103 - Blackburn & Burnley
1:25,000
Explorer 19 - West Pennine Moors

ACCESS *Start from Sunnyhurst Wood's Lychgate car park. Bus service from Darwen centre. This is signposted along Earnsdale Road, off the A666 on the northern edge of Darwen. The car park is just off the road junction where Sunnyhurst Lane becomes Tockholes Road. If starting from the main road (Darwen-Blackburn buses), an alternative approach avoiding the road is detailed below. Darwen has a station on the Blackburn-Bolton line. A further alternative start is Roddlesworth information centre, mid-route (see start of WALK 13).*

An easy walk to a famous landmark. Glorious heather, woodland and outstanding views (and a couple of well placed pubs).

S Sunnyhurst Wood was largely created in the 19th century to provide cover for game birds. In 1902 it was acquired by public subscription to commemorate the Coronation of King Edward VII. In the hands of the local authority, this extensive parkland/woodland makes a fine public place of recreation on the edge of Darwen. A visitor centre is encountered near the end of the walk.

NB: If starting from the main road, follow Earnsdale Road and take the footpath opposite Salisbury Road down into the woods. This leads upstream to the visitor centre, where the latter stages of the main route are joined.

From the car park return along the road to the *Sunnyhurst* pub.
Despite its florally attractive frontage this is perhaps just a little too
early to break the walk! Further temptations are found across the road,
with various refreshments available at the licensed tearooms. **Directly
opposite the pub an enclosed footway rises between buildings,
quickly climbing onto broad heathery verges.** Already, Darwen
Tower beckons directly above, while looking back there is a big view
over the sprawl of Blackburn to Bowland and Pendle Hill beyond.

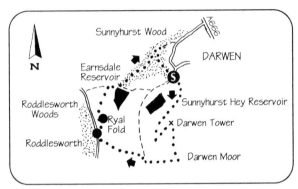

**At the top the track enters a corner of Darwen Moor, and with the
tower hovering above, there is an immediate choice. Though the left
fork is more direct, better to opt for the right one. This runs a superb
slanting course across the steep, heathery flanks.** One can now reap
the benefits by fully savouring the sweeping views. Immediately
below, and not particularly superb, is Sunnyhurst Hey Reservoir of
1875. Far more attractive is Earnsdale Reservoir (1854), at a lower
level in a bowl of trees beyond it. The dome of Great Hill is seen ahead
beyond Roddlesworth Woods, while a good half of Lancashire is on
parade from the flatness of the Fylde to the bumps of Bowland.

At the top a level path is met running along the moor edge. Directly
ahead are the masts atop Winter Hill. **Turn left for five minutes to the
beckoning tower.** Dwarfed beneath this 86ft/26m structure is an
Ordnance Survey column standing at 1220ft/372m. At this very
moment Darwen itself suddenly appears, dominated·by its town
landmark, the India Mill chimney. Built in 1867 by mill-owner Eccles
Shorrock, the 300ft/90m, square chimney is in the style of a Venetian
belltower. Remarkably, it has been used as a nesting site by Peregrine

falcons. Darwen Tower (properly the Jubilee Tower) was built in 1897-98 to commemorate Queen Victoria's Diamond Jubilee, but more meaningful to many is its celebration of the re-opening of Darwen Moor to the public two years earlier (see page 58).

The tower was fully restored in 1972 after falling into disrepair. 25 spiral steps lead to a lower viewing platform, which might prove far enough on a windy day! A further 40 stone steps precede 17 metal ones to reach a door opening out onto the bracing upper platform. Three plaques affixed to help identify features of the view serve only to confuse, until it dawns that, bizarrely, all the features are 'back to front'! Distant features identified include such far-ranging mountains as Snowdon, the Langdale Pikes and Kinder Scout. Nearer to home are many features of the West Pennines, with Winter Hill and Holcombe Moor (with the Peel Tower prominent) the most obvious.

Numerous well made paths radiate from the tower. Leave by the one heading directly south across the moor (in line with the mast on Winter Hill). In August 1995 the moor was the scene of a disastrous fire. Damage was deep as a result of continued underground burning for several more weeks, and the sterling efforts to extinguish it were then to be matched by efforts to restore the ground cover.

The path runs broadly on to rise gently to a T-junction. Here turn right for a level walk over the heathery watershed. At the end another path junction is met in front of a fence junction. Take the stile in front and descend the slender fence-side path. This quickly meets a broad path on a hairpin overlooking Stepback Clough: continue down to a forlorn ruin, Old Aggies. Properly Stepback Cottage, the name refers to an earlier resident murdered in 1860. Occupied into the early 20th century, there was a happier period when the cottage served refreshments.

At the fence behind, double back down a short path to a lower stile to meet a broad trackway below. Go left on this, over the stream and out through the trees. There is a good view over Earnsdale Reservoir and back across to the tower. At the end, take the right-hand gate/stile, and a grassy cart track descends the large pasture to arrive at the colourful Hollinshead Terrace. These houses are a surviving reminder of a former mill that stood on the site beyond (see page 59). A kissing-gate admits onto the road. Advance the few yards out to the bus turning circle and Roddlesworth information centre.

Purpose built in 1996, the information centre serves a very popular corner of the West Pennine Moors, and has small displays of local interest, with toilets attached. The adjacent *Royal Arms* is a multi-roomed gem, of which sadly fewer and fewer remain: it also boasts an enterprising range of beers from the local independent brewery, Thwaites of Blackburn.

Leave by a rough road on the other side of the pub, leading to the hamlet of Ryal Fold. Turn left on the drive into a farmyard. Ryal Farm on the right dates from the 17th century, displaying mullioned windows and a gabled north front somewhat hackneyed by later additions. **From the gate at the end an enclosed track leads out into a field. Follow the right-hand boundary for a contrastingly pleasant stride to the very far end, passing through a gorse corner to a small gate onto a junction of ways.** This is a historic spot as we enter Dean Lane, a former packhorse route from Tockholes to Darwen. **Turn down the setted way (known as Donkey Brow) to the right to emerge onto the end of the Earnsdale Reservoir embankment.**

Don't cross the embankment, just cross the access road to a gate into Sunnyhurst Wood. A good path heads away, and an early fork presents a choice. Opt for the left branch which runs an undulating course along the top of the wood. When it eventually starts a marked descent it quickly reaches the first fork of note (alongside one of the wood's many seats). Here continue downhill to meet the valley path alongside a paddling pool where stone arch bridges abound. Across it is the main carriageway through the woods. Quite a number of memorial stones and tablets can be spotted within the woods.

A detour just two minutes to the left will lead to the visitor centre and refreshments. A tearoom and shop occupy the big house built in 1911 to celebrate the Coronation of George V: a stone tablet tells a little more. Refreshments are also served from a kiosk attached. Just past it, Sunnyhurst Wood's visitor centre occupies a former gamekeeper's cottage, fronted by a lovely cottage garden. Inside are local interest and natural history exhibits. If returning to the main road simply continue downstream, keeping left at two forks to emerge onto the road by way of Falcon Avenue. **The main route resumes on the drive up the valley floor, past the pool to reach a former bandstand. Here turn sharp left up a broad path, climbing sometimes steeply above Sunnyhurst Clough to a T-junction. Go left for two minutes to a woodland entrance gate just yards from the start.**

Darwen Tower

12

RODDLESWORTH WOODS & ABBEY VILLAGE

START *Tockholes*   *Grid ref. SD 665214*

DISTANCE *5¼ miles*

ORDNANCE SURVEY MAPS
1:50,000
Landranger 103 - Blackburn & Burnley
1:25,000
Explorer 19 - West Pennine Moors

ACCESS *Start from Roddlesworth Information Centre car park, by the Royal Arms on the Blackburn-Belmont road south of Tockholes village. Served by bus from Darwen, Blackburn and Belmont (and Sundays from Bolton). An alternative start is Abbey Village on the A675 Preston-Bolton road, at the foot of the walk: this is served by bus from Chorley and Blackburn.*

A good mix of woodland, brook, reservoir, fieldpath, bridlepath, history, pubs and views. The opening section, as far as the head of Roddlesworth Upper Reservoir, coincides with Roddlesworth Nature Trail, for which an informative leaflet is available.

S Purpose built in 1996, Roddlesworth information centre serves a very popular corner of the West Pennine Moors. It has small displays of local interest, and toilets. The *Royal Arms* is a multi-roomed gem, of which fewer and fewer remain: it also boasts an enterprising range of beers from the local independent brewery, Thwaites of Blackburn.

From the car park go left to the bus turning circle then cross to the gates into Roddlesworth Woods. A broad way slants down to the left, soon narrowing and descending very pleasantly through a clearing.

Below it we encounter the now sodden course of a road built in 1883 from Halliwell Fold Bridge to transport coal by horse-drawn waggons to Hollinshead Mill (see page 59). **At a fork go left to quickly arrive at the stone arched Halliwell Fold Bridge.**

Cross the bridge and take a kissing-gate on the right to head downstream, enjoying the company of the river Roddlesworth (better known locally as Rocky Brook). The happy stream tumbles over gritstone slabs, and in springtime the woodland floor is a carpet of bluebells. The woods cover something like 200 acres, and contain a splendid mix of trees. The natural tree cover was augmented from 1904 by plantations by Liverpool Corporation, who had acquired the area for their reservoir building plans.

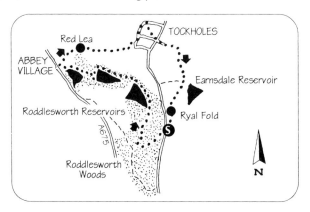

The super walk leads down to a concrete bridge, which is crossed to soon reach a fork. Go left (nature trail signs), soon arriving at a seat and good viewpoint over Roddlesworth Upper Reservoir. This is the highest of three neighbouring reservoirs built in the mid-19th century, all of which we shall encounter. A 3½-mile drain known as the Goit was built to transfer their water to the more extensive water catchment facilities at Rivington. The Goit is visited during WALKS 1 and 2. **Continue on the thinner path along the bank, over a bridge and soon rising to meet a firmer, broad path. Go left on this, dropping down to cross a sidestream then rising markedly towards the wood top. The way runs along here for some time, during which a track merges from the left. The way ultimately slants down to cross the dam of Roddlesworth Lower Reservoir.**

The open embankment gives a good view back over the water to Darwen Tower. **At the end follow the access track out to a ford and bridge on the outflow. Cross to the old reservoir keeper's house, taking a snicket up its side to rejoin the access road. This leads out along the embankment of Rake Brook Reservoir to meet the road alongside the *Hare & Hounds* pub in Abbey Village.** Abbey Village is a designated conservation area, its long rows of mill cottages lining the main road being a reminder of days when the weaving mill meant everything to this community. It operated from 1846 until 1971, the village's sole employer. The name 'abbey' is thought to date back to links with Whalley Abbey. There is a second pub, the *Royal*, and a shop and a Post office along the street.

Leave without actually touching the road, by an access road from a gate/stile on the right. The drive descends to a large house (Bensons Farm). Here swing right down a concrete track into the wooded clough. Towards the bottom take a stile on the left to access a footbridge over the brook. Slant right up the other side to a stile into the garden of an old house. Pass to the right to a gate in front, to be faced by Red Lea Farm. This superb old house bears a 1674 initialled datestone.

Again pass to the right, along to a stile onto a field track. Follow this up to some pens at the top. From a stile on the left rise to another just above, then slant up to the top left corner of the field. Pass to the right of an attractive pond and along to a corner stile. Now go left up a grassy enclosed way to arrive at the mini hamlet at Higher Hill, on the edge of Tockholes. The main house, last on the left, is a rambling old place with numerous mullioned windows. **As the drive climbs away, take a squeezer stile on the left and cross the field to a stile onto another rough road. Follow this right past Ivy Cottages and onto the road, Chapels Lane.**

Go left, passing Tockholes United Reformed Church. Dating from 1880, it replaced an early non-conformist chapel. On the right, the narrow Long Lane offers a simple short-cut. **Chapels Lane continues on to pass Chapels Farm.** This is yet another old house, dating from the 17th century, again with mullioned windows. **Just ahead is St. Stephen's church.** The gateway arch leads to a surprising modern place of worship replacing an earlier building. The stone building on the right bears a tablet identifying it as the old school of 1834. A stone pulpit stands attached to the foot of a window.

Opposite Chapels Farm take a gate with a tumbledown stile alongside. Head up the field to a stile at the top, then left to another and steeply up to a gate/stile. Rise past the cottages and Tockholes Post office onto the main road. Tockholes, as we have seen, is a very scattered community. The Post office is housed in the former Wall Bank Cottages of 1612. If thirsty there are pubs 100 yards either way, *Rock Inn* to the left, *Victoria Hotel* to the right.

Turn right past the village hall and then sharply left at the crossroads, up the rough road of Weasel Lane. This lead past houses and runs on to a lone large house. Darwen Tower occupies the skyline ahead, resembling a space rocket ready for launch. **Along the front of the house (note the deer painted on the side wall) the way continues as a bridleway, dropping gently down to a track junction.** This is a historic spot as we enter Dean Lane, a former packhorse route from Tockholes to Darwen. **Take neither option but use a small gate in the wall in front. A thin path runs on through an attractive gorse corner.** Down to the left nestles Earnsdale Reservoir, with Darwen Tower dominant on the moor behind.

Simply follow the fieldside along to its tapering end, where an enclosed way leads to the farm at Ryal Fold. Ryal Farm on the left dates from the 17th century, displaying mullioned windows and a gabled north front somewhat hackneyed by later additions. **Bear right on the drive heading out, and just before the pub a stile on the left is the key to another stile back into the car park.**

Red Lea Farm,
Tockholes

13

DARWEN MOOR

START *Tockholes*   *Grid ref. SD 665214*

DISTANCE *5 miles*

ORDNANCE SURVEY MAPS
1:50,000
Landranger 103 - Blackburn & Burnley; Landranger 109 - Manchester
1:25,000
Explorer 19 - West Pennine Moors

ACCESS *Start from Roddlesworth Information Centre car park, by the Royal Arms on the Blackburn-Belmont road south of Tockholes village. Served by bus from Darwen, Blackburn and Belmont (and Sundays from Bolton).*

The heathery delights of Darwen Moor offer a simple walk with panoramic views.

❺   Roddlesworth information centre has small displays of local interest, and toilets. The *Royal Arms* is a multi-roomed gem of which sadly fewer and fewer remain: it also boasts an enterprising range of beers from the local independent brewery, Thwaites of Blackburn.

Darwen Moor occupies a precious place in the history of the access movement. Though not remembered in such national terms as Kinder Scout, it was nevertheless a significant scene in the struggle to regain old rights. Many of the public paths on the moor began as coal miners' trods, but were closed by the Lord of the Manor in 1878 on the pretext of upsetting his grouse shooting. Local folk set about a long campaign to walk the moor again, and by 1896 free access was declared. Later that year thousands enjoyed a grand procession over the moor to celebrate the return of their rights, and today it remains an urban common, where the public have a right to roam at will.

From the visitor centre follow the road left past the bus turning circle to Hollinshead Terrace. These former millworkers' cottages are surviving evidence of Hollinshead Mill, which stood here until demolished in 1905 by Liverpool Corporation, who had acquired the land for water gathering purposes. It operated less than 50 years, and today it is hard to believe that at its peak up to 150 people worked here. **Pass to the right of the houses to a kissing-gate into a field, and a grassy cart track rises away.** Over to the left are super views of Earnsdale Reservoir, with Darwen Tower on the moortop above.

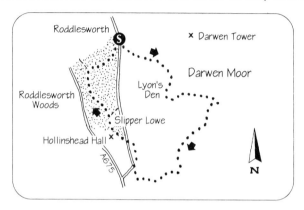

At the top an enclosed way runs under trees into Stepback Clough. At the bend don't cross the brook, but take the first stile on the right, from where a track heads away. A white stone across the stream marks the location of the shaft of a former coal mine, one of numerous on these moors. **The stream is soon crossed to find a nice little fall over a great slab of rock. The way rises pleasantly out of the part wooded clough and onto the open moor.** Darwen Tower re-appears back to the left on the skyline.

A stand of trees is reached marking Lyon's Den. This is said to be the site of a cottage occupied two centuries ago by a local character of immense stature, John Lyon. **The path curves up to meet a similar path at an incongruous seat: turn left.** At once Darwen Tower becomes the focus of attention: this famous landmark is the focal point of WALK 11. The skyline beyond features Pendle Hill and Bowland's moors, while further west is Preston and the low country of the Fylde. Back over our right shoulder the massive mast on Winter Hill appears.

At a watershed fence abandon any designs on the tower by forsaking the main path for a slimmer one branching right past another seat. This soon broadens and runs a grand course through the heather. The wide views ahead feature Holcombe Moor and Peel Tower, with rolling South Pennine moorlands layered beyond. **The path declines gently to another junction. Here double sharply back right to cross the upper reaches of Duckshaw Brook.** The heathery embankment is evidence of a small dam constructed to serve mine workings.

The path rises gently away and runs on to another moortop fence. Winter Hill is straight ahead now, rising above a vista which is presently one vast moorscape. **Over the stile, the ways fork: either will suffice as they meet a long half-mile further. The main one goes straight on, bound for Winter Hill ahead. It meets a broader path to turn right with it and a crumbling wall to reach an old gateway. The right branch offers more interest as it runs past two former mineshafts.** Both are crudely fenced but have caved in over the years leaving little to see. As the heather is left behind, the light green path stands out clearly among darker moor grasses. **At the end the path curves left to rejoin the main path just short of a gateway in an old wall.**

This is an inspiring moment, as the ground falls away steeply with Great Hill and Winter Hill rising across the trough of the A675. This spot is marked by a well-sited seat and a weathered Peak District & Northern Counties Footpath Preservation Society guidepost, 1960 vintage (illustrated on page 3). Now the less cumbersome Peak & Northern Footpaths Society, this organisation celebrated its centenary in 1994, and though its attractive guideposts proliferate in the Peak District, it is nice to see them pointing the way in this region also.

Pass through the gateway and descend the grand path, crossing the small stream and shadowing it down to merge into a Landrover track. Continue down this to a stile off the moor. A green track (now a drain) slants down the field to meet a firm cart-track. This is the former Bolton-Preston coach road, long superseded by the modern road. **Go right to approach a bend of Crookfield Road. Without joining it, take a bridle-gate on the right, and a concession bridleway curves away up the field.** Courtesy of North West Water, it is well constructed and a fair improvement on the road. **It runs above a small wooded bank then curves back down to the road. Cross straight over and a narrow footpath slants down into Roddlesworth Woods, quickly arriving at the site of Hollinshead Hall.**

60

Hollinshead Hall was the manor house of Tockholes, and though dating back to the 14th century, today's ruin is of the 18th and 19th centuries. A large part of the extensive house was demolished in 1776, to be rebuilt on a much less grand scale. It was bought in 1835 by Darwen mill-owner Eccles Sharrock, but was soon in disrepair and demolished by Liverpool Corporation. The site was restored in 1983, and an information board includes a plan of the layout of the site.

Greatest feature of interest is the easily missed Well House, in a corner back up to the right. This was restored first by Liverpool Corporation and again in the 1970s by conservation volunteers. It houses a lion's head water spout and three stone troughs, carrying water from no less than five separate springs. It is thought the water spout and plaque above it may have come from an earlier building, its origins possibly linked to the worshipping of a holy spring. Certainly the supply and the powers of water were more greatly valued in centuries past.

Continuing, a broader path runs on through the trees, rising right to meet the bend of a broad cart track. Slipper Lowe car park is just along to the right. **Our way keeps straight on the track.** An early detour is along a thin path rising left onto the grassy knoll of Slipper Lowe. This affords the finest prospect north over the substantial Roddlesworth Woods to the Bowland Fells and Pendle Hill. Between them on a clear day the more distant delights of Ingleborough and Penyghent are the noblest shapes to be seen within the Yorkshire Dales. Darwen Tower is also revealed to the right.

The track, meanwhile, runs down into the woods. Known as Mill Lane, this is still the route of the coach road. **Never claustrophobic, the latter stages of the descent pass some fine beech trees and enjoy the company of the lively river Roddlesworth (known locally as Rocky Brook) before reaching stone arched Halliwell Fold Bridge.**

Don't cross the bridge, but take the footpath on the right. An alternative is to follow the concession bridlepath initially, soon turning right on a lesser fork at the top of a rise (here are scant remains of the farm of Halliwell Fold), then merging with the direct path. **The path rises steeply then runs more pleasantly and unfailingly on up to the start.** En route we cross the overgrown and moist line of a road built in 1883 from Halliwell Fold Bridge to transport coal by horse-drawn waggons to Hollinshead Mill; the path also encounters a delightful clearing decorated by some heather.

14

GREY STONE HILL & CALF HEY

START *Hoddlesden*   *Grid ref. SD 715222*

DISTANCE *9 miles*

ORDNANCE SURVEY MAPS
1:50,000
Landranger 103 - Blackburn & Burnley
1:25,000
Explorer 19 - West Pennine Moors

ACCESS *Start from the village centre. Served by bus from Darwen and Blackburn. there is ample considerate street parking. An alternative start, mid-route, is the Calf Hey car park off the B6232 Blackburn-Haslingden road (bus service also).*

This lengthy walk features several rougher sections. Allow ample time and don't consider it as a family or genteel ramble.

S Hoddlesden is a hilltop village high above Darwen, and though extended with modern housing, its centre is an attractive arrangement with some old weavers' cottages by the war memorial in Queens Square. Across the street is the *Ranken Arms*, outside which is a Silver Jubilee millstone. There are a couple of shops and Post office. Mining on the slopes above the village was once sufficient to have a two-mile branch from the railway at Darwen built to take out the coal.

Leave by Bayne Street opposite the pub. Passing Queens Square it runs down to the school and the hidden St. Paul's church. Pass left of the school and along a carriageway leading to a cemetery. Keep straight on through it to join a rough road. Turn down it to a road, go right a few yards and then left along a reservoir embankment. At

the far end a stile admits into a field. **Rise away with the wall to a corner then turn up the wallside to the top corner. Rise left with a sunken way, entering it at a stile part-way up, to arrive at Shorrock Fold.** Over to the left, Darwen Moor and its tower are seen beyond the reservoir. **A makeshift stile leads into the garden: turn right, up past the house to a stile onto the drive. Continue up to a bend at another house.**

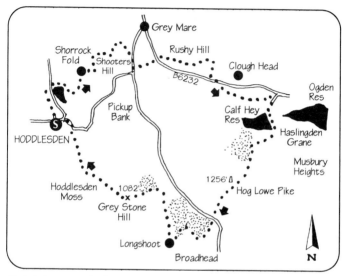

Go left between the houses. Keep left of a fence to follow the top side of a field away, with a sunken way forming (the track/lane suggested on the map has long gone). At the bend at the end take a stile to the right and climb steeply with a fence. At the top keep straight on to merge with a low wall from the left, under Shooters Hill. A deep, part-wooded valley is revealed, with a reservoir glimpsed down to the left. Only the pylons spoil this lovely corner. **When the wall ends, cross the stile in a fence and a thin path slants down to the tiny stream. Cross it just short of an old wall coming down, immediately above the impasse of a waterfall (not easily viewed).**

Another sunken way doubles back up out of the trees. Rise to a stile in the fence above, then slant up the pasture. On the brow pass left of the pylon and on through a collapsed wall. Keep straight on (bound for another pylon) to the low but extensive remains of a farmhouse. Through the crumbling wall behind, a broad green track slants gently right, passing below another pylon to a gate/stile onto **Broadhead Road.** The *Grey Mare* pub is a few minutes along to the left. **Turn right for two minutes, and just before a junction take a stile on the left. Rise up the field, past a ruin to reach an old wall corner. Keep on up the wallside to a wall/fence junction at the top. Advance with a substantial wall to the B6232 Blackburn-Haslingden road.**

Cross straight over and across a field towards a red brick shelter, joining a reedy old way in front of it. Turn right to escape into open pasture under Rushy Hill. Now simply advance along the wallside with the valley of Haslingden Grane outspread. Excellent views are now revealed of the valley (see also WALK 16). **This splendid march continues until just short of a second plantation, where a stile in the wall sees us meet the Rossendale Way. Head down the large pasture to a stile back onto the road. Cross with care and go left on the verge.**

The Rossendale Way quickly turns right, but continue 50 yards further to a stile, where a splendid green way slants away. Passing the abandoned pastures of Haslingden Grane, it soon becomes enclosed and charts a good course along the valley side. Views over the valley feature Hog Lowe Pike (on our route) on the skyline. **The way latterly descends more steeply to debouch onto a narrow road. Turn right (or use a parallel path through the trees) to quickly reach a fork at an old burial ground.** This is all that remains of a Methodist chapel of 1815 (closed in 1955). On the left is a bird hide in the woods.

Hog Lowe Pike,
looking to
Winter Hill

The right branch leads to the popular Calf Hey car park. This is on the site of the houses of Grane village. Haslingden Grane was a part of the Forest of Rossendale, a medieval hunting forest until 1507. At the turn of the 19th century the valley was home to 1300 people, but within a few short years it became a ghost valley as the residents were moved out, victims of the water board's need for 'unpolluted' water. Calf Hey Reservoir was constructed between 1854 and 1859, and the larger Ogden was added between 1903 and 1912. The latter reservoir submerged two former mill sites and spelt the death knell for the valley's surviving residents.

Pass through the car park and down a rough road. As it swings right at the bottom, take a bridle-gate on the left and descend the surfaced path to the dam of Calf Hey Reservoir. A salvaged 'gate valve' of 1856 is proudly displayed en route. While crossing, note the numerous abandoned trackways zigzagging up the facing slope.

Across the dam, ignore the broad track and take a stile on the left. A path climbs the pasture to a stile onto a contouring path (the Rossendale Way again, very briefly). Follow this right, and within 100 yards take a thin but clear branch left up through the heather. This runs a contouring course above the lower path and reservoir. Reaching a small clough, cross it to a stile and away just a little further to a crossroads of green paths. Double back left to climb to the fence, following this up to emerge overlooking the deep side valley of Hog Lowe Clough.

The path runs between fence and edge, soon encountering a modern flagged section. Continue on to a fork. A popular branch (not the right of way) goes right, crossing the upper limits of the clough to a fence-stile, thence rising clearly to the Ordnance Survey column standing at 1256ft/383m on Hog Lowe Pike. Possibly an ancient burial mound, this offers grand views all round, with Winter Hill dominating.

The left branch advances to its own stile, then crosses less obviously to the waiting skyline saddle. From it go right, 50 yards up past a gate in the wall to find a stile. Across, slant away down the large rough pasture, aiming for the left side of the plantation ahead. In the bottom corner pass through an old wall and descend to the abandoned farm below. Pass to the right and out in the company of the old drive onto Broadhead Road.

Cross to a stile opposite and head down the fieldside outside Broadhead Plantation. Keep on until the trees end, then take a stile in the fence. Rise up the reedy pasture still outside the plantation, reaching a pool and a ruin of something once substantial on the brow. Here a stile gives access to the plantation. On entering, turn immediately left and down the side, at the bottom corner going down a few yards further to join a rough road. Turn left down this to cross the stream and leave the plantation, the road rising by heather banks to approach Longshoot Farm.

At the gate don't enter the yard, but take a stile up to the right. Cross to the far corner of this enclosure, and from the stile head away from the farm on a rough path on the line of a ditch and bank. Almost at once the white house at Pastures appears ahead, a useful guide. The path runs on the moor edge and through the remains of a wall. The treetops of another plantation appear ahead to replace the one on the right, which is left behind. Nearing Pastures the path drops down to cross the dry head of the clough, and rises to a gate where a reedy way runs on to the house. Don't take this, but slant back across the reedy hollow, with an old wall leading to the plantation corner.

Enter the plantation at a stile and head up the left side to a stile back out. A thin trod now runs across to the top of Grey Stone Hill. A fence comes up from the right and its bend marks the highest point at just over 1082ft/330m. In the latter yards heather takes over, and the view of the western slopes is one of a fine purple hue in late summer. The Grey Stone is hard to distinguish, there being quite a number in the summit environs, none being too distinctive, most being across the stile.

Cross the stile and aim north-westerly towards a low depression (Hoddlesden housing beyond). Keep generally to the edge of the heather above the less inviting Hoddlesden Moss on the left. Soon some grouse butts appear, drop down to them to meet the line of a Landrover track. This leads down past the ten butts, now with a small clough on the left. At the bottom a stile leads off the moor. Turn right with the fence heading away, at the end joining an enclosed farm drive. Turn right on this, running a straight course down to a small group of houses. A choice of finishes awaits, the easier way being to turn right out onto the road, and left to quickly finish. Alternatively turn left to a gate, from where an overgrown way descends to a stream, there turning right to return to the edge of the village.

15

OSWALDTWISTLE MOOR

START *Oswaldtwistle*   *Grid ref. SD 742253*

DISTANCE *6¾ miles*

ORDNANCE SURVEY MAPS
1:50,000
Landranger 103 - Blackburn & Burnley
1:25,000
Explorer 19 - West Pennine Moors

ACCESS *Start from a viewpoint car park on the A677 Blackburn-Haslingden road, 1½ miles south of Oswaldtwistle. Two alternative starts are: A) Just off-route at Clough Head Information Centre on the B6232 Blackburn-Haslingden road, served by Haslingden-Blackburn bus; B) The Shoulder of Mutton at Green Haworth, served by bus from Oswaldtwistle.*

A tasty dip into the valley of Haslingden Grane, mixing colourful pastures with rougher moorland. There is little climbing involved as the walk remains relatively high throughout.

S The start point features picnic tables and a view indicator. Very varied features of interest are identified, with the hills of Bowland, Longridge and Pendle backed by the higher Three Peaks country of the Yorkshire Dales. Nearer to hand are some urban landmarks. **From the car park rejoin the road and walk west/right for a couple of minutes. Cross with care at the dip to where two paths head off to the left within a few yards of each other. These present an immediate choice, and will soon rejoin on the climb towards the moor.**

The first climbs as a grassy drive towards the forlorn ruin of Brewer Lot Farm. It ends abruptly, and with potential danger, at a dramatic landslip with a 20ft drop at our feet into Warmwithens Clough. With

the ruin over to the left, a thin path advances up the rim to quickly reach a delightful waterfall. Cross the stream, climb the steep bank to the top corner of the wood, then pass through the crumbling wall immediately above. The map shows the path entering and leaving the wood, but in the absence of stiles it makes greater sense to keep outside the fence to the end. As it drops away, cross with a raised mound to a difficult gateway in a wall, onto a rising cart track.

The second and easier option remains on the road over the bridge, and from the stile a path heads upstream. Keep to the higher path at the early fork, rising above the side clough with a fence. When it meets a wall take a stile at the junction and head away along the wall-side, reaching a stile at the end onto a rising cart track. Turn up this by the wallside.

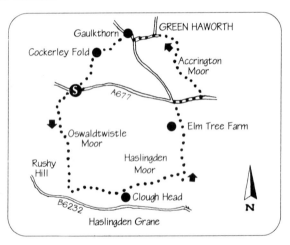

Both routes re-united, head up this good wallside track, through a gate and up towards Oswaldtwistle Moor. As the wall turns away, the green track winds up to the corner of a grassy dam. Don't expect any water, however, as the abandoned Warmwithens Reservoir has been reclaimed by the vegetation of rough pasture.

Use the bridge to cross the old concrete outflow, then bear left on a thinner path along the side of the old reservoir. At a fence, the way is signed off to the right, as opposed to the line taken on the map.

Initially pathless, slant through reeds to gain a pronounced ditch slanting to the skyline. A faint path rises with this, and an old wall comes in to make firm company as a small rise is topped. The scant ruins of Higher Warmwithens are glimpsed just over to the left. **Now simply follow the old wall to its terminus on the peaty moortop. A large cairn marks the end of the wall, after which a few less salubrious minutes ensue.**

Maintain the same southerly direction over the flat, wet watershed with little trace of the path. Poor visibility should pose no problem, as the path and wall we are aiming for cannot fail to be joined at some point. Ahead, the moorland skyline across Haslingden Grane slots into place, with the rounded Hog Lowe Pike prominent. To our immediate left is the rolling Oswaldtwistle Moor, as the walk's highest point is gained on this flat morass, at about 1200ft/366m. It is a little disconcerting to hear the sound of nearby traffic, for the busy B6232 Blackburn-Haslingden road is surprisingly close, though we don't join it.

Quickly dry ground returns, and a pronounced little edge is gained on firm grass at the scant ruins of a farm. The road is seen just below, and also now a better appreciation of the valley of Haslingden Grane. See WALK 16 for more on this once thriving, now abandoned valley.

The path slants down to join a path running along the wallside below, with a small plantation behind. Turn left on the clear path, and simply remain on here as it makes a long contour around the base of the moor, on past the next small plantation. Just prior to this second plantation, the route of the Rossendale Way is joined for rather less than a mile and a half. Emerging beyond the trees, there is a better prospect of the valley, with Ogden Reservoir and the smaller Holden Wood Reservoir seen beyond. The car park at Clough Head also appears just below, as unfortunately also does the Heap Clough Quarry. **At the wall corner after the plantation a wallside path branches right to descend to Clough Head.** Clough Head Information Centre is operated by the West Pennine Moors Countryside Service. There is an exhibition of the valley's history, refreshments and toilets.

The walk resumes along the same line as before, on with a reedy, sunken way through two more pastures to a group of trees. There are sweeping views over the valley to the opposite flank, featuring the chimney at the old quarry on Musbury Heights, and the pudding top of Hog Lowe Pike. On again, the still active Heap Clough Quarry is just below now. From the ruin beneath the trees continue on the green way of the old drive, and just past the next smaller ruin the path is nudged left onto a parallel trod, with numerous old causey stones revealed. Maintain the contour on to an oddly sited footbridge. With the quarry now behind, the path descends steeply into Deep Clough, to a grassy embankment and footbridge alongside old, more traditional quarry workings.

The path climbs out of Deep Clough to another ruin, and from its solitary tree head away with a low wall on the left. Through a gateway at the end, slant down to the right corner and go right along the wallside. Pass through a large gap in it and resume a little further past ruins to meet a firm track at the head of a wooded clough. Here begins the return north over the watershed of Haslingden Moor. Turn sharply left up this cart track: part way up the Rossendale Way turns off right at a couple of trees. Continue straight up, the grassy track soon levelling out to run along to a gate/stile onto the moortop.

The moorland return is, however, no repeat of the earlier crossing, being a very swift and much drier affair. Head away across the moor, quickly gaining the low point of the watershed, with the view north rapidly embracing Elm Tree Farm, just ahead. Bearing right, slant down with a reedy, sunken way to a gate off the moor: this is found to the right of the big pasture in front of the farm. Descend a broad enclosed way to join the drive, and remain on this as it drops down to meet Haslingden Old Road at a T-junction.

Go right for a short half-mile on the grassy verge, then turn left down an enclosed farm road, just short of an isolated house on the Hyndburn-Accrington boundary. Remain on this to its terminus, ignoring other farm drives branching right. At the end the way emerges via a gate/stile onto a corner of Accrington Moor. Follow the track away, soon veering right with a fence across the edge of the colourful centre of this rough pocket moorland. The track swings right past a reedy pond to meet a farm drive at the far corner, with Green Haworth golf course over the wall.

Go left on this rough road alongside the golf course. Accrington is well seen outspread down to the right. Passing the clubhouse the road leads out onto a through road. Go left for a few minutes to a junction at the *Shoulder of Mutton*. En route we pass the appealing Green

Haworth Lodge set back on the right. This settlement at Cross Edge features the gaunt Green Haworth Wesleyan Chapel rebuilt in 1903, as well as the handily sited pub.

Turn right down the footway of the winding road, and leave at the first chance at the first buildings on the left at Gaulkthorn. Take the drive doubling back into a farmyard. Note the large stone water trough and the tablets on the barn, dated 1884. **At the end turn right down an enclosed green track.** This enjoys good views over this side valley which is to return us to the start point. **At the bottom use a gate on the left to resume down the wallside. At the bottom, a footbridge lead over the pleasing wooded clough. On the other side bear right on the path slanting away from the clough.** The stream engages in some lively waterplay in a double bend as we leave it. **The thin path rises to a stile into the environs of Cockerley Fold at the top corner.**

Joining the drive, go right into the central yard, in front of the main house. Keep straight on to a free-standing stone barn ahead, past that to a gate alongside a concrete building. Having left the farm, head along the fieldside towards the plantation ahead, and after a gate, a clearer path slants left up to an outer wall corner. Down to the right is a good sized pond, with Oswaldtwistle in the valley below. **From the gate/stile turn along the field bottom, passing along the top side of the wood. At the highest point, after a second tiny stream, strike up the field centre on a faint way leading to a stile onto the A677, with the car park just yards to the right.**

Waterfalls,
Warmwithens Clough

16

HASLINGDEN GRANE

START *Clough Head*   *Grid ref. SD 751231*

DISTANCE *6¼ miles*

ORDNANCE SURVEY MAPS
1:50,000
Landranger 103 - Blackburn & Burnley
1:25,000
Explorer 19 - West Pennine Moors

ACCESS *Start from Clough Head Information Centre car park on the B6232 Blackburn-Haslingden road, 2½ miles west of Haslingden centre. Served by Haslingden-Blackburn buses.*

A straightforward circuit of the valley of Haslingden Grane, with easy walking and fine views over the reservoirs and moors above. Much of the walk is along the route of the Rossendale Way.

S Clough Head information centre is operated by the West Pennine Moors Countryside Service. There is an exhibition of the valley's history, and refreshments and toilets. Haslingden Grane was a part of the Forest of Rossendale, a medieval hunting forest until 1507. At the turn of the 19th century the valley was home to 1300 people, many in small weaving communities. But within a few short years it became a ghost valley as the residents were moved out, victims of the water board's need for 'unpolluted' water. Today, countless old farmhouses are little more than piles of stones amid pastures gone to seed.

A concession footpath starts at a stile immediately to the left of the information centre. A path climbs to another stile, then steeply up a wallside to meet the route of the Rossendale Way. Back along the valley side is the noise of the large Heap Clough Quarry. **The Way, with its numerous waymarks, is now followed until further notice.**

Turn left over the stiles and shadow the sturdy wall contouring away beneath the slopes of Haslingden Moor. Over the wall are good views of the valley, featuring Calf Hey and Ogden reservoirs. **After passing a plantation a stile is met. Cross and descend the large pasture to a stile onto the B6232. Cross with care and go left on the verge a few yards, then escape right along a green way.**

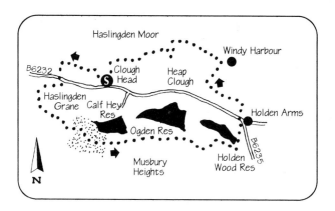

Beyond a stile the path swings right and runs dead straight. The way remains clear as it swings left before a wall corner and on around the dalehead. As the track bears right just short of some low ruins, keep straight on a thin path past the old farm to accompany a reedy, deep-sunken way. Calf Hey and Ogden reservoirs are now well seen down to the left. **The path drops down to a sidestream, which is crossed on the right.**

The broad, old walled way rises away opposite, but leave it almost at once as the path is signed through a gap in the wall on the left. The faint path contours across to a Withins-like ruin, and on to another. The clearer path runs enclosed by old walls past a crumbling wall junction to a more substantial ruin at a small clough. Pass to its right and down to the stream crossing. The path rises behind and takes a stile into a young plantation. The path runs on above more mature trees to emerge at a superb vantage point over the valley. A Peak & Northern Footpaths Society sign confirms the route of the Rossendale Way, while a seat by a small quarry site overlooks a scattering of trees and the reservoirs: a good place to linger.

The path winds exquisitely down into scattered woodland, fading a little just before dropping onto a broad, firm path. This is the route of the Calf Hey Trail, for which a leaflet is available. **Go right on this, almost at once over a footbridge on a sidestream. Take the upper path heading away, and at the next bridge at the foot of Hog Lowe Clough, keep on the upper path again. It runs on above a stand of Scots pine to a pair of stiles and footbridge into open country.** Above, hugely colourful flanks overlook the reservoirs. Calf Hey was constructed between 1854 and 1859, and the larger Ogden was added between 1903 and 1912. The latter reservoir submerged two former mill sites and spelt the death knell for the valley's surviving residents.

Stay on the path above Ogden Reservoir until just past a ruined farm. Above are tumbling fans of spoil from the old quarries on Musbury Heights. Ahead, Holden Wood Reservoir appears: lowest of the three, it was completed in 1897. **At a stream crossing the path forks. Leave the Rossendale Way by a grassy path angling down to the left before running on above the dam wall to meet the lower section of a former tramway.** Quarried stone was lowered down the incline to a short branch of the now defunct Accrington-Stubbins railway. It went off to be used as setts, kerbs and flagstones: the quarry closed in the 1920s.

Keep on to a gate just beyond, with a white farmhouse (Tenements Farm on the map) ahead. Don't pass through, but turn up the fenceside and then left with the fence along the base of the hill. Just before a lone house take a stile in the fence and slant down to a ladder-stile just below. Descend the field to a similar stile in the bottom corner, below some trees, and turn right along the farm road. It leads above Holden Wood Reservoir and swings across the dam to lead out onto the wide road junction (B6232/B6235) west of Haslingden. Handily placed is a comfortable pub, the *Holden Arms*.

Turn left along the Blackburn road as far as the church. St. Stephen's was rebuilt here after removal from Grane in 1927: today it is currently an antiques shop, with a cafe. **Cross the road and up a drive outside the cemetery. At the top pass through a gate to the right of the cottages, and go right to a barn. Here a deep sunken way rises left to a gate/stile.** Above, note the good job done planting new trees on the spoil of more quarries. **Heading away, as the path forks remain on the level one with the wall. Passing through several stiles it emerges onto a farm road. Continue on this, climbing steeply to approach Cloud Hill Farm, named Clod Farm on the map.**

Pass to the right and follow a fence away to a stile in the field corner. **Head away with a fence to a stile onto a track west of Windy Harbour Farm. Here the Rossendale Way is rejoined. Go left on this clear, level route along an upland shelf, passing above a plantation.** Distinctive across the valley is the knoll of Hog Lowe Pike. **With Heap Clough Quarry appearing ahead, the improving path reaches a T-junction with a green track just after a tree-fringed ruin and a stile.** The enticing track is an old way crossing the moors to Oswaldtwistle (see WALK 15). **Turn left down it just as far as an old quarry site on the left and the head of a wooded clough.**

Double back right past a ruin, quickly passing through an early gap in the wall on the left and on to another gap just ahead. Bear left up the field to a stile and gap, then head away left with the low wall on the right. This leads to another ruin and its lone tree, with the quarry just ahead now. A path descends steeply to a footbridge in Deep Clough, at the edge of old quarry spoil. Cross the edge of the spoil on a drained dam and up the steep slope behind. At a curiously sited footbridge rise gently left, with the quarry fence now very close on the left. The thin path runs on past ruins, becoming a part paved way, merging into an old green track to pass another ruin. This super, formerly walled way leads to a tree-shrouded ruin, and at last the quarry is behind.

From the stile after the ruin there are alternative finishes. Turn down to a stile below, from where a good path runs down through a young

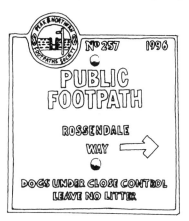

plantation to adjacent stiles at the bottom. Go right with the fence, then deflected left of a small wood (not quite as per map). A track forms to run on to re-enter Clough Head car park. Otherwise, remain on the Rossendale Way until meeting the outward route a little further.

Footpath sign above Calf Hey Reservoir

MUSBURY CLOUGH

START Helmshore   Grid ref. SD 778214

DISTANCE 6½ miles

ORDNANCE SURVEY MAPS
1:50,000
Landranger 103 - Blackburn & Burnley
Landranger 109 - Manchester
1:25,000
Explorer 19 - West Pennine Moors

ACCESS Start from the Helmshore Museum of the Lancashire Textile Industry on the B6214, a mile south-west of Haslingden. Car park adjacent. Served by bus from Haslingden; also from various towns further afield on Summer Sun/BH Monday. The East Lancashire Railway (preserved line, Bury-Rawtenstall) is a good half mile off-route near the walk's end.

A magnificent excursion on excellent paths around the heads of two deep cloughs in the folds of Rossendale.

⑤ The absorbing Lancashire Textiles Museum is housed on two adjacent sites, the water-powered Higher Mill of 1789 and Whitaker's Mill of 1860. This is a perfect location to chart the development of the textile industry, as Lancashire was of course world famous for cotton spinning. Working exhibits include a steam engine of 1846, and there are examples of two renowned Industrial Revolution breakthroughs, Hargreaves' Spinning Jenny and Arkwright's Water Frame. There is also a cafe and a shop, and the museum is open from April to October.

From the mill entrance first look up the road to a solitary chimney in a field across the road. **Begin by turning left along the road, passing the red-brick Park Mill. Immediately after a short terrace of cottages**

turn right in front of a works building. Keep right on this small road as it bridges Musbury Brook, rising, now as a rough lane, by a row of houses. At the end turn sharp left after a car park and head along the farm drive, which leads unerringly along to the houses at Carr Lane. At once we are away from industrialisation: during this stage Musbury Tor forms a fine aspect up to the left, with its minor gritstone fringe.

Pass to the right of the houses on the track which bridges the stream and quickly ends a little further upstream. Take a gate/stile on the left onto a green way shadowing the brook, a lovely corner as a grassy stone arched bridge is reached just beyond. Take a gate/stile in front and follow a fine green track along the floor of the pasture, parallel with the brook.

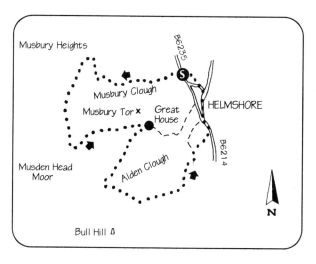

Rising at the end to a gate/stile, the track climbs right above a reedy, drained millpond. Keep right as the track forks, climbing outside the wooded confines of Hare Clough. Part-way up it swings left to rise between old walls to the first long-abandoned farm of the day. Once a delectable spot in a fine setting, it was abandoned decades ago like several more soon to be encountered. This is a grand viewpoint for the clough, at the heart of a medieval deer park created for the Lords of Clitheroe.

77

The green track doubles sharply back, and as the track swings up left, keep straight on a fainter way with the old wall to return to the head of Hare Clough. Cross and rise away from converging walls on a thin, clear trod up the slope behind. In the company of a reedy ditch, rise past an old wall and onto gentler ground. Bear left on a near-level path coming in, and rise to a sturdy wall corner above. Just yards along the wall-side a stile is met, and the course of the Rossendale Way encountered. Though our way is left, first look over the stile to see the remains of a corner of Musbury Heights Quarry. This once extensive site produced the stone for untold setts, kerbs and flags for the growing towns before closing in the 1920s.

From the stile a clearer path strikes left across the grassy moor, to commence a superb traverse around the head of Musbury Clough. With all the work done, settle down to enjoy this classic stride: small wonder the Rossendale Way chose to take in this corner of the district! The Rossendale views are on a big scale, though the rugged image of Musbury Tor is tempered somewhat by the flat green field on its top. The path simply runs around the hillside on a near-level march.

The path quickly reaches the former farm of Rushy Leach before continuing on, past another then slanting down to cross a stream. Just before it, note the lovely waterfall visible just upstream. The green path then runs on to the next Withins-like ruin before encountering the twin southerly feeders of Musbury Brook in quick succession. The ruins of a stone hut with compartments are passed midway.

Re-emerging above another ruin, the path now leaves this valley and angles gently up onto a brow. Faintly crossing an old ditch and wall, it runs clearly on to a ladder-stile/gate into a contrasting green field. Before moving off, a clear day will reveal some peaks of the Yorkshire Dales beyond the bold outline of Pendle Hill, to the north. Best discerned when snow-capped in winter (or on the occasion of this research, snow-capped in May!) are Whernside and Ingleborough.

Resuming, a broad green track slants across the field at the very back of the tamed Musbury Tor. The track runs unfailingly on, past a stand of hardy sycamores and down to approach the environs of Alden Clough. As a concrete track it drops down towards extensive agricultural buildings at Great House. Ahead now are new valley views over the clough into the main valley of the Irwell. At the gate above the farm, don't go further but instead take a ladder-stile on the

right. For a quicker return, do neither but go left on the top side of the wall to follow paths and lanes back to the start. **Angle back on a path joining the drive below, and follow this rough lane past two houses to end at a third, Fall Bank Farm.** With its surviving habitations and lived-in look, Alden Clough makes a striking contrast to the neighbouring Musbury Clough.

The path by Musbury Brook, early in the walk

Rise right of the house to a wall-gap, on to a stile beyond, then along the field top. The deep folds of Alden Ratchers await, with the upper slopes of Bull Hill on Holcombe Moor directly ahead. **After a further stile head faintly on past a ruin, a better path forming to reach a stile onto moorland.** Here we enter the National Trust's open country of Holcombe Moor. **A grand path runs on to cross the two arms of the brook, each offering charming waterfalls in amongst colourful terrain.**

After the second waterfall the path angles away, becoming a broader track as it slants up the base of the moor, on the slopes of Bull Hill. Rising to a wall-corner, the highest point of the walk is reached at about 1148ft/350m. The view north extends to embrace Buckden Pike and Great Whernside, two massive fells of Wharfedale. A Peak & Northern Footpaths Society guidepost presides over this path crossroads, and only now does the Rossendale Way part company.

Our way turns left, on a good green track shadowing the wall down the edge of the grassy moor. At the bottom corner take a gate off the moor and head down a walled bridle-track. Almost at once we pass Robin Hood's Well, a curious shaped stone above a spring with the sound of running water below. The local civic trust have marked the spot with a plaque. Final views of Ingleborough and Pendle Hill are on offer.

Our restored way, Moor Road, drops down to join a drive. Either go left down this to run down to the main road (B6214), or take the small gate immediately opposite. This sends us along a field top to be level with the big house of Dowry Head, from where turn left down the field-side. Follow this boundary down to a gate onto the B6214 opposite some cottages. Cross to the footway and turn left for just a minute or so to a main junction by the *White Horse* pub. On the grassy sward stands an old guidepost, inscribed *To Haslingden 1¾ miles & 255 yards to the Towns gate.*

Do as directed and swing down to the right, descending to a bridge alongside the substantial stream emerging from reservoir-choked Haslingden Grane. Across it stands a fine clock tower in the public park. Keep on the road to the *Bridge End* pub, and crossing Bridge End Bridge, turn sharp left on Station Road (also known as Bowl Alley). As the road bridges the beck, keep straight on a footway beneath modern houses, and this heads pleasantly upstream. Note the architecturally interesting slim, four-storey terrace opposite.

The path is soon nudged away from the beck by a large works' car park, and rises to embrace the former Accrington-Stubbins branch line. Within minutes its leafy course is interrupted by steps at a bridge. Here bear left on a path re-entering the museum car park. Ice creams are usually available, so treat yourself! If something stronger is needed, the *Robin Hood* pub is just north along the road, by a former railway viaduct.

18

HOLCOMBE MOOR

START *Stubbins*   *Grid ref. SD 781183*

DISTANCE *6¾ miles*

ORDNANCE SURVEY MAPS
1:50,000
Landranger 109 - Manchester
1:25,000
Explorer 19 - West Pennine Moors

ACCESS *Start from the National Trust's Stubbins Estate car park (easily missed) on the B6214 between Holcombe and Helmshore. The main road below is served by Ramsbottom-Haslingden buses.*
•ACCESS NOTE - This walk crosses the MOD's Holcombe Ranges, and a crucial section cannot be undertaken when red flags are flying: see page 8. Much of the walk is on National Trust open country.

A bracing stride around the slopes of Bull Hill, on an uneasy mix of National Trust and Ministry of Defence land: fine upland scenery.

❺ The Stubbins Estate comprises of 436 acres between valley and moor, and was acquired by the National Trust in 1943. In 1994 a further 916 acres of Holcombe Moor were acquired from the Ministry of Defence. **From the car park a permissive path runs north alongside the road, quickly emerging just short of a farm drive. Turn left up it for a very steep pull to the farm at Chatterton Close. At the top go right along a rough lane, emerging onto National Trust open country by the top of Buckden Wood.**

Just a little further, a broad, enclosed track branches up to the left alongside the spoil heaps of Ironstone Delph. Take this, becoming fainter as it scales a narrow strip of rough ground descending from the moor. Part-way up when the ways part, take the fainter right

branch slanting to the top right-hand corner of these diverging walls. The increasing views reach north to Pendle Hill and beyond, and down the valley over Haslingden.

Emerging onto Holcombe Moor, bear gently right up easy grass slopes, crossing over a path and curving up to locate a thin path. On the brow, at a stake, this further improves (with a view back to the upper section of Peel Tower), and runs around to a wall corner. This crossroads of footpaths is marked by a Peak & Northern Footpaths Society guidepost. The view north from here is outstanding, a clear day revealing Yorkshire Dales peaks from Whernside and Ingleborough to Buckden Pike and Great Whernside.

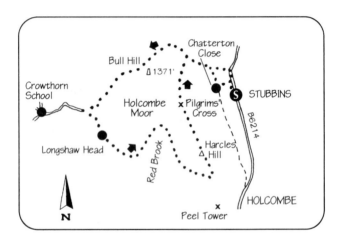

Our way goes left, a thin but clear path rising gently across the moor. Steadily and faintly it breasts the grassy upper slopes of Bull Hill to reach a minor saddle in the watershed. The TV mast on Winter Hill appears ahead. **On the highest point of the path a row of MOD warning signs is seen on the left, and just above them stands a flagpole.** From the flagpole it is less than a hundred yards to the Ordnance Survey column marking the summit of Bull Hill. Although this uppermost part of the hill is neither on rights of way nor access land (the National Trust boundary ends at the MOD boundary) it has always been a popular objective, assuming a red flag is not decorating the flagpole.

At 1371ft/418m Bull Hill is the second highest summit on the West Pennine Moors. The view is very extensive, and on a clear day in May I was privileged to see snow in four National Parks (highlighted) in amongst an upland panorama including **Snowdonia**, Winter Hill, Black Combe beyond Morecambe Bay, though much of the **Lake District** is hidden behind the Forest of Bowland, **Yorkshire Dales** (including Three Peaks country), Pendle Hill, the South Pennines, Holme Moss TV mast, and the tops above Glossop in the **Peak District**. For a severe pruning of the route, one might continue south-east on the path heading away from the trig. point to descend to the Pilgrims' Cross path crossroads within just a few minutes.

The main path resumes along the base of the summit mound, quickly reaching an MOD sign. At this point the path bends markedly right to embrace the unappealing moist moorland. The name Wet Moss on the map just north of here itself spans a wide area, and is suitably descriptive! The path is clear and other than after a spell of wet weather, a decent pair of boots should be enough to keep feet dry.

After a less than enamouring 20 minutes during which time eyes are forlornly turned back to the receding green knoll of Bull Hill (and with the Winter Hill TV mast ahead), things improve and the path runs on to a crumbling wall corner on the edge of the moor. Head on with the right-hand wall, turning left at the end on a track that zigzags down to a works building, following its rough access road down onto a junction at the head of a surfaced road.

Here double back left on a broad track running along to Longshaw Head. During this spell there are good views over to Entwistle and Wayoh Reservoirs. The upper one is surrounded by plantations while the latter features an impressive railway viaduct and some attractive natural woodland: the village of Edgworth nestles in front. All this is backed by Winter Hill, its moorland skyline running north to an abrupt end at Darwen Tower. **A cart track continues beyond the buildings to run along the base of the moor.** Now we have extensive views south-west over the suburbia of Bury. **As the track turns a corner the top half of Peel Tower appears ahead, and another flagpole and MOD notice are reached. If you've got this far then the flags are not flying, so continue on the suddenly improving green way which swings in towards the characterful head of Red Brook. This cracking path slants in to the main stream crossing amidst rugged clough scenery.**

Immediately on crossing the stream, a less obvious **upper path** offers a parallel option to the main one, both running round to a lesser stream then contouring back out the other side of the valley head. The upper path runs on to a crossroads with a broader path climbing at angles. The main path runs delightfully on to an MOD sign and flagpole, thus leaving the range for NT land. Just yards further, take the branch doubling back up to the left. Part-way up its reaches a crossroads with a lesser path (the higher-level option from earlier).

The easiest way is to continue up the main path, easing out on the moortop to run alongside MOD signs to the Pilgrims' Cross (as in WALK 19). **For greater interest, turn right along the thinner branch path, running on beneath a line of small quarry scars and traversing round to swing up onto the moortop. Merging unconvincingly with another path, the way runs along by a minor trough with the grassy flank of Harcles Hill to the left.** Ahead, the upper section of the Peel Tower is revealed. **Keep on as far as a crossroads with a broader path, with Harcles Hill Farm now visible ahead, to the left.**

Red Brook, Holcombe Moor

84

The Peel Tower is now just minutes away to the right, and well worth a visit if not saving it for WALK 19. The return route, however, turns left, a path quickly climbing to find a sprawling cairn on the summit of Harcles Hill (1217ft/371m). This grand viewpoint lists Whernside, Ingleborough, Pendle Hill and Holme Moss alongside countless other northern hills: ahead, the Pilgrims' Cross is clearly seen across the moor. The whole of the Peel Tower is now visible behind. A good grassy path continues northwards, bound for Bull Hill. Skirting a minor knoll the path rises gently to a crossroads to intercept the footpath to Helmshore at the Pilgrims' Cross. The stone we see today imparts the following information about this lonely moorland route.

ON THIS SITE STOOD THE ANCIENT PILGRIMS' CROSS, IT WAS EXISTING IN AD 1176, AND PROBABLY MUCH EARLIER. PILGRIMS TO WHALLEY ABBEY PRAYED AND RESTED HERE. NOTHING IS KNOWN OF THE REMOVAL OF THE ANCIENT CROSS, BUT ITS MASSIVE SOCKETTED FOUNDATION STONE REMAINED HERE UNTIL AUGUST 1901.

IN AD 1176 AND IN AD 1225 THE PILGRIMS' CROSS IS NAMED IN CHARTERS OF GIFTS OF LAND IN HOLCOMBE FOREST. IN AD 1662 KING CHARLES II GAVE THIS MANOR TO GENERAL MONK, DUKE OF ALBEMARLE THROUGH WHOM IT HAS DESCENDED TO THE PRESENT LORD OF THE MANOR.

THIS MEMORIAL STONE WAS PLACED HERE MAY 24TH 1902 BY THE COPYHOLDERS OF THE MANOR AND OTHERS.

On the Pilgrims' Cross, Holcombe Moor

The view is also worth noting before moving off: the top of Peel Tower overtops Harcles Hill, while in distant terms, a clear day still offers Snowdonia, the Peak District and the Yorkshire Dales. Turn right on the footpath shadowed by a line of MOD warning signs. Directly ahead is Pendle Hill, with Buckden Pike and Great Whernside divided by the big masts on Hameldon Hill, above Burnley. The path runs on beneath one last flagpole and an array of signs, then drops towards a wall corner. Turn down to the right here on the strip of land that brought us up to the moor. Retrace outward steps, but for variety, when level with Buckden Wood, a National Trust concession path uses a ladder-stile into the trees to descend the hugely attractive beech-wooded clough onto the road. Go right to finish.

19

PEEL TOWER

START *Holcombe*   *Grid ref. SD 781162*

DISTANCE *4¾ miles (5 via Bull Hill)*

ORDNANCE SURVEY MAPS
1:50,000
Landranger 109 - Manchester
1:25,000
Explorer 19 - West Pennine Moors

ACCESS *Start from the Holcombe Moor/Peel Tower car park on the B6214 at Holcombe, above Ramsbottom. Bus service a few minutes away at Ramsbottom and Holcombe Brook. • ACCESS NOTE: The optional detour onto Bull Hill is on MOD land - see page 8.*

Easy moorland walking through splendid scenery, dominated by the mighty Peel Tower. The walk is almost entirely on National Trust land.

S   The old settlement of Holcombe remains a small community at the base of Holcombe Moor, astride the old Bury-Haslingden road. Its numerous buildings of character include cottages used in the late 17th and 18th century by handloom weavers. Some are seen on the very last leg of the walk. The National Trust purchased the Holcombe Moor estate from the Ministry of Defence as recently as 1994.

From the car park the tower very much dominates things, and in no time at all we will be stood alongside it. **Cross the road to find a permissive fieldside path rising onto a cobbled back road. Turn right on this to a junction at a spring, then double back left on the rough road onto the foot of the moor. Almost at once take the branch right, which after an initial bend makes a sustained slant across the face of the steep, colourful moorside.** Several more direct footpaths break off it, but if not wanting to break sweat remain on this gently angled access track. This gives ample time to savour the big views over the Irwell Valley: there may be much industry on the valley floor, but there's certainly plenty going on, and the hillsides beyond remain relatively unspoiled.

At the top the track doubles back and the drive swings in to Top o'th'Moor Farm, while a broad path runs on the couple of minutes to the waiting tower. The Peel Tower (or Holcombe Tower) really is a massive monument. Over 120ft high, it was built in 1851 to commemorate Sir Robert Peel. Born in Bury in 1788, as Prime Minister he saw through the repeal the corn laws (making bread cheaper); though is perhaps more commonly known as the founder of the modern police force, hence the nickname 'peelers' (and later 'bobbies'). The tower is normally open at weekends and bank holidays: an admission charge is made to climb to the top.

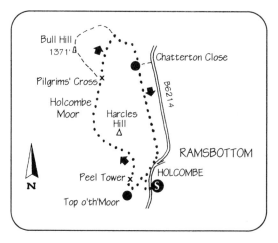

Leave not by the main moor-edge track, but by a path heading north across the moor past the deep crater alongside the tower. This runs on to a fence-stile then continues north, meeting a crossroads with a thinner path just short of a saddle in front of Harcles Hill. Though one could continue straight over Harcles Hill (see WALK 18), more interest awaits by turning left across the flat moor. Towards the end views open out over the valley of Red Brook, and across the intervening moors to Winter Hill.

Approaching steeper flanks below, the path forks into two thin branches. Take the trod bearing right to trace its gentle curve around the moor, dropping only slightly before contouring round above the valley of Red Brook, with the grandeur of its upper reaches on Bull Hill outspread. Picking up a couple of slanting old ways from the left, the trod traverses along beneath minor quarrying scars to a crossroads with a broader path coming up from below, by a flagpole. An MOD warning sign here is the first of many that will shadow the next section: fear not, we don't enter the danger area. Turn right up this, enjoying grand views into the upper reaches of the clough. At the top a contrastingly different scene awaits as the broad path runs on across Holcombe Moor to reach the Pilgrims' Cross.

The informative stone we see today occupies the site of an ancient pilgrims' cross on this lonely moorland route: see WALK 18. **The stone marks a crossroads of paths, and a choice of routes awaits. The main path runs straight on with the MOD signs, soon passing beneath a flagpole and dropping to a wall corner. Turn down to the right here, descending between converging walls to leave the moor and join a farm track at the bottom alongside the modest spoil heaps of Ironstone Delph.**

The crossroads at the Pilgrims' Cross is with a path climbing from Harcles Hill to continue to the summit of Bull Hill. If the MOD range is not in use, then a very inviting and easy option is to bear left up this path which rises very gently and quickly to the Ordnance Survey column on Bull Hill: this appears shortly after the flagpole that stands behind it. For more on Bull Hill, please see WALK 18. Note that the diversion onto Bull Hill is not a right of way, but is a popular path - when firing isn't taking place!

Leave by crossing the short distance to the flagpole and dropping down the pronounced slope to locate a thin path crossing the moor. Turn right on this, gently angling down to a wall corner, and a crossroads with broader ways at a Peak & Northern Footpaths Society guidepost. Turn right along the level moorland path, and from the brow it slants down, increasingly faintly, towards another wall corner at the head of a strip of rough moorland descending off the moor. A thin, broadening path drops down between converging walls to join a firm track at the bottom alongside the modest spoil heaps of Ironstone Delph, by which time we are back on the main route.

Turn right along the broad track to quickly reach the farm at Chatterton Close. Keep straight on past the buildings to a gate at the end, from where the open moor is re-entered. A good cart track runs along its base, becoming a firm drive at the next house, Higher Tops. The rough lane soon slants down from the base of the moor as the enclosed Moor Road, with the church spire in view ahead. Remain on this until at the bottom it meets the main road, conveniently opposite the *Shoulder of Mutton* pub.

It is not actually necessary to join the road, for just yards short of it we can keep on a slim cobbled back road past a very characterful old house on the right (this features mullioned windows and a weathered inscription on the side). Just beyond, another back road is joined, running parallel with the main road. This leads past more of Holcombe's chatacterful properties. At the end the outward route is rejoined just two minutes from the start.

The Peel Tower, Holcombe Moor

89

20

TURTON TOWER

START *Jumbles Country Park*   *Grid ref. SD 736140*

DISTANCE *6½ miles*

ORDNANCE SURVEY MAPS
1:50,000
Landranger 109 - Manchester
1:25,000
Explorer 19 - West Pennine Moors

ACCESS *Start from Jumbles Country Park car park by Jumbles Reservoir, just off the A676 Bolton-Ramsbottom road. The main road is served by bus from Bolton, Bury and Rawtenstall. Bromley Cross station on the Bolton-Blackburn railway line is less than a mile away. An alternative start, en-route, is Entwistle embankment car park (see WALK 21): this would save a mile by omitting the start/finish from Jumbles Reservoir. A further start is Turton Tower on the B6391, which is served by bus from Bolton.*

❺ Jumbles Country Park occupies a very popular location within the Bradshaw Valley. The modern visitor centre is operated by the West Pennine Moors Countryside Service, and includes an exhibition of local and natural history. There is also a tea garden and toilets. Encompassing some 55 acres, Jumbles Reservoir was completed as recently as 1971. A leaflet describes a circular trail around the reservoir, detailing numerous features of interest.

From the information centre follow the rough road north along the shore of Jumbles Reservoir. Part-way along, a short path climbs away to see a former millpond. **At the reservoir head cross the tall concrete bridge.** There is great geological interest in the quarry face at the reservoir head here, but you'll have to read the leaflet to make any sense of it. **Head away past a Peak & Northern Footpaths Society**

guidepost up the stepped path into the trees. Emerging at the top it rises past a lovely pond (with Chapeltown church spire as backdrop) and descends past a pillbox to join the B6391. The concrete pillbox was one of some 25,000 built as defensive measures during the Second World War.

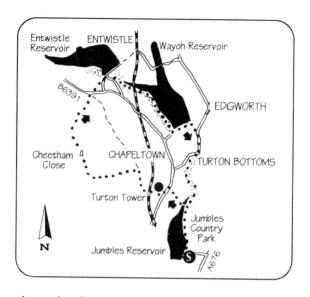

Cross the road and tramp the footway left for a few minutes, then turn on the drive to Turton Tower. Turton Tower was built as a pele tower around the start of the 15th century, a popular form of defensive house. The immensely attractive black and white farmhouse was added in Elizabethan times, with further additions in the 19th century. The house passed to the local authority in 1930 and is open to the public. Internal exhibits include 17th century arms, and furniture. There are also nine acres of woodland and a shop and tearoom.

Keep straight on the cart track past the hall. Next features of interest are a 19th century waterwheel from a nearby mill, restored alongside a barn; and an elaborate castellated railway bridge. This was so built at the whim of the owner of Turton Tower, using the new railway to pass through his land as an excuse to create a dignified 'folly'. The left-hand tower has steps leading up to a seated viewing platform.

The track climbs away from the railway bridge then turns right to run along a field bottom. Locate a stile on the right after a clump of trees, signifying the arrival of a path from the mill down below. This path crossroads marks a choice of ways. An easy alternative to the impending Cheetham Close is to remain on the track above Turton Tower, leading on to Clough House Farm and continuing out along its drive to rejoin the full route at the B6391.

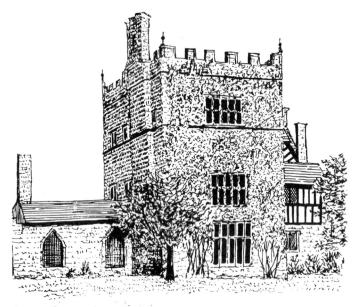

Turton Tower

For the main route, take the thinner path rising left up the field centre. Above a stile it rises left of a shed and up through the small wood. Exiting at the top, the thin path rises away. There are now extensive open views, southwards to the Manchester metropolis, and back right to Holcombe Moor. The path meets the wall on the left, with the watershed just ahead. Ahead looms the mast decorated crest of Winter Hill, looking very close indeed. Cross the fence-stile and take the path rising right, along the marshy moortop of Cheetham Close to the isolated Ordnance Survey column.

At 1079ft/329m this marks the summit of the walk. The name Cheetham is derived from Chetham, Humphrey Chetham having at one time been the owner of Turton Tower. Belmont village shelters, as ever, under Winter Hill, while to the north Turton Heights is the continuation of our own high ground. To its left is Turton Moor, while to the right Hog Lowe Pike and the Peel Tower flank either end of Holcombe Moor. The tower is impressively overtopped by the shapely tilted summit of Knowl Moor across the Irwell Valley. **Resuming, a small standing stone on the right is the pointer to a handful of ancient stones.** Almost lost in the rough grass, these are the scant remains of a prehistoric stone circle probably marking a burial site.

The path continues across the moor, dropping to a stile and then along to a crossroads with a broader path in a hollow. In front stands an old white iron Bolton Corporation Waterworks boundary post. Turn right here, the improving path slanting left down to the bottom corner of the enclosure. From the corner stile the path drops down to a lone sycamore sheltering traces of a ruin at Three Lowes. Bear left between the rounded knolls and the path reaches a stile. Entwistle Reservoir appears below in its shroud of trees.

An improved path runs down to join the B6391 Greens Arms Road. Go right a few yards to a stile on the left, and a path runs down to cross the drive to Entwistle embankment's upper car park. The path itself then runs down into the car park. From here another path drops down onto the road at the dam of Entwistle Reservoir. This attractive tree-choked sheet of water was began in 1831 and enlarged in 1840, and though named Turton & Entwistle Reservoir on the map, it is universally known simply as 'Entwistle'. An easy hour's circuit of it can be enjoyed as an optional extra (see WALK 21). If a pint is needed, the *Strawbury Duck* at Entwistle is just a few minutes along the dam and the rough road beyond.

The route doesn't cross the dam, but turns down into the main car park. At the far end a stile sends a concession path downstream, joining a broader one to lead through the woods. The western arm of Wayoh Reservoir appears below, and the path, mostly downhill, passes under Wayoh Viaduct to reach a junction. The path left crosses an embankment which affords a good view of the reservoir and the tall arches supporting the Blackburn-Bolton railway (illustrated on page 97).

Resume downstream on the main path, leading unfailingly through woodland to the dam of Wayoh Reservoir. As is ever the case, a tablet ensures the names of the august waterworks committee are preserved for prosperity. **Cross the embankment road and a path runs along to the right to emerge onto the road at Turton, rather handily alongside the *Black Bull* pub.**

Turn right down the footway, passing a Post office and couple of shops. Just before the bridge at Turton Bottoms, take the penultimate road left (Birches Road), a cobbled street. Old cottages abound i:. this once thriving industrial area. **As the road swings left to bridge the stream, bear right past a house to find a footway leading to a stone arched bridge on Bradshaw Brook.** Pack Saddles Bridge is built very much in the style of a packhorse bridge, dating from the late 17th century. Today it has railings added for safety, while alongside is a surviving ford. **Joining a back road (Vale Street), go left, becoming cobbled again to pass housing and re-cross the stream again.**

On this open ground the old road swings right, still cobbled, but at once seek out a footpath even closer to the stream. This it shadows down through a deep wooded gorge. Passing a water installation the way becomes a rough road leading back to the bridge at the head of Jumbles Reservoir. Conclude the walk as it began.

Pack Saddles Bridge

94

21

YARNSDALE

START *Entwistle*   *Grid ref. SD 721171*

DISTANCE *4¾ miles*

ORDNANCE SURVEY MAPS
1:50,000
Landranger 109 - Manchester
1:25,000
Explorer 19 - West Pennine Moors

ACCESS *Start from Entwistle embankment car park, on Batridge Road off the B6391 Greens Arms Road north of Bolton (most easily reached from the A666 Blackburn-Bolton road). Entwistle station (Blackburn-Bolton line) is half a mile away, on the route. Edgworth-Bolton-Darwen-Blackburn buses also run within half a mile of the station.*

A very undemanding extended circuit of an upland reservoir, with several even shorter options. By turning this into a straightforward reservoir circuit, the distance can be halved.

❺   From the main car park cross the road and take a broad path along the south shore of Entwistle Reservoir. The reservoir was began in 1831 and enlarged in 1840. Though named Turton & Entwistle Reservoir on the map, it is universally known simply as 'Entwistle'. While the reservoir remains enshrouded by a cloak of conifers, this is nevertheless a pleasant, relaxing start by banks of bilberry, heather and bramble. **Towards the end the tapering head leads to a foot-bridge on Cadshaw Brook.** By crossing here, the shortest option will lead back to the dam along the indented north shore.

A good path continues upstream to a second footbridge (and ford). At this point a half-mile loop awaits, following a concession path into the recesses of Yarnsdale. Simply continue upstream through the

trees, soon opening out to reveal Cadshaw Rocks ahead. This is marked on the map as Fairy Battery, and is said to have been the location of illegal non-conformist services during the 17th century. It is perhaps better known in modern times as a playground of rock climbers. This is a delightful enclave, seemingly far from anywhere yet within half a mile of the busy A666. **As the scene opens out, a path forks down to the right to cross a footbridge on the stream.**

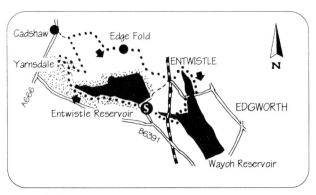

A stile on the left gives access to the crag, but our way returns downstream, this time on a contrastingly narrow path hard by the water's edge. Just yards short of the middle footbridge, take a stile on the left by the plantation corner, and a thin path slants up the pasture. As it fades, keep straight on to meet a broad green track. Go left on this, gently rising to join a rough road at Lowe Hill. With the buzz of the main road to the left, we happily turn right, enjoying long easy strides as it rolls on over the high ground. This old route linking Cadshaw with Entwistle has mercifully been spared 'improvement'.

The immediate surrounds are largely green fields rather than pastures gone to seed, as might have been expected. More distantly, Holcombe Moor and the Peel Tower are seen ahead, with the South Pennines behind. Turton Heights rise to the right above the plantations, while Winter Hill stands to the rear, westwards. Part way along, Entwistle Reservoir appears shimmering below. **In time the old road descends past a heather reclaimed quarry at Edge Fold, down as a colourful sunken way to a junction of access roads. Turn right on the narrow rough road (Edge Lane) which leads to the pub at Entwistle.** En route, note an initialled 1689 datestone incorporated in a ruin on the right.

Entwistle is a curious spot hidden away from the outside world, yet in fact very civilised with the *Strawbury Duck* pub and a railway station. The pub is a highly popular walkers' rendezvous, and has for many a long year served an impressive range of good beers. At the foot of Edge Lane stands the hugely attractive New Hall, with its datestone from the 1700s. For a quick finish, simply pass round the side of the pub and follow the rough road (Overshores Road) back to cross the dam.

The full route crosses the road bridge over the railway and descends 75 yards down the road to a small gate on the left. A path drops down from the gate into dense woodland, falling to a junction in front of a footbridge. Cross the bridge and the ensuing one over Broadhead Brook, from where the path turns downstream. It quickly parts company from the stream, and the head of Wayoh Reservoir takes over below. The path runs on to meet the Entwistle road just ahead. Like Entwistle before it, Wayoh Reservoir was built to supply Bolton, and it enjoys a setting much favoured by birdlife. It was opened in 1876, and its capacity was doubled in 1962.

Cross the embankment and leave the road by a kissing-gate on the left. A super concession path leads by the wooded reservoir shore, swinging round to another embankment bridge. This one is a public footbridge, and it carries us over the western arm of the reservoir. To the right rise the massive arches of the Wayoh Viaduct, carrying the Blackburn-Bolton railway high above the water and woods. **Across, turn right on another concession path which rises through woodland under the edge of the viaduct and back to the car park, branching right off a broader track where signed just short of the end.**

Wayoh Viaduct

BROADHEAD CLOUGH & WHITTLESTONE HEAD

START *Entwistle*   *Grid ref. SD 721171*

DISTANCE *5 miles*

ORDNANCE SURVEY MAPS
1:50,000
Landranger 103 - Blackburn & Burnley (tiny section)
Landranger 109 - Manchester
1:25,000
Explorer 19 - West Pennine Moors

ACCESS *Start from Entwistle embankment car park, on Batridge Road off the B6391 Greens Arms Road north of Bolton. A start from Entwistle station (Blackburn-Bolton line) is on the route, and saves about a mile's walking. Bolton-Edgworth-Darwen-Blackburn buses also run within half a mile (and on the route itself, at Grimehills).*

An intriguing ramble with a variety of scenery and terrain, visiting an absorbing site of industrial archaeology.

❸ **From the car park rejoin the road and cross the embankment of Entwistle Reservoir.** The reservoir was began in 1831 and enlarged in 1840, and though named Turton & Entwistle Reservoir on the map, it is universally known simply as 'Entwistle'. **At the far end a private rough road runs on to the waiting white-walled pub.** En route we pass a camping barn and a red brick terrace. Entwistle is a curious spot hidden away from the outside world, yet in fact very civilised with the *Strawbury Duck* pub and a railway station. The pub is a highly popular walkers' rendezvous, and has for many a long year served an impressive range of good beers. At the foot of Edge Lane stands the hugely attractive New Hall, with its datestone from the 1700s.

Cross the road bridge over the railway and after 75 yards take a small gate on the left. A path descends into dense woodland, falling to a junction in front of a footbridge. Don't cross, but take a stream-side path up to use a higher footbridge. The path heads away, and soon leaves the stream in order to climb an old way between undergrowth on a distinct spur. Emerging, follow the fence up the spur, crossing it at a gate part way, to approach the houses at Wayoh Fold (Wayoh Farm on maps). Some nice woodland decorates the valley on the left. Take a stile left of the first house, and on through the yard of this restored mini hamlet and out onto the road.

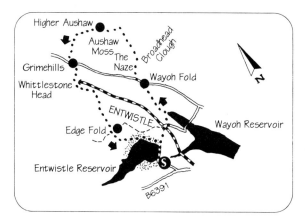

Go left 100 yards then take a grassy, redundant drive on the right. At the top it emerges into the open and splits several ways. Take the more inviting right branch of the upper two tracks, a good green way slanting up beneath the Naze. Broadhead Clough forms the large valley on the right, looking back down it to Wayoh Reservoir. The skyline behind us is broken by the ubiquitous summit of Winter Hill.

Levelling out, the track passes the head of a small clough made more colourful by the rubbish tipped about. On through a gateway, the dark holes of some coke ovens can be seen: a large group is visible lower down the slope, while a pair can also be seen directly ahead. Keep straight on the peaty path, crossing another faint way to arrive along a reedy way at the prominent ovens site. These noteworthy remains of beehive style, stone built coke ovens still have their insides charred black from years of use long ago. Back down to the right, the larger collection can easily be seen: keen eyes will detect both sets of ovens marked on the map by circles. Possibly 200 years old on this prominent hilltop site, they used coke from locally won coal to smelt iron in an efficient manner.

From these upper ovens double back left up a faint way onto the moortop. Bear left to a gateway in the watershed fence on Aushaw Moss, then turn right with it. The sweeping upland skyline to the west ranges from Cheetham Close, Turton Heights, Winter Hill, Turton Moor to Darwen Moor, with Darwen Tower prominent on the end. **Cross the edge of a surprising green upland pasture surrounded by heather moorland, and giving the marshy fence corner ahead a wide berth, continue on to a fixed gate at the far end.**

Entering a better moorland pasture, the path runs on to join the remains of a wall, which leads pleasantly along the heather moorside. At the end, next to heather recolonised quarries, the path drops down through a gateway off the moor towards the house at Higher Aushaw. Keep straight on down the green lane to join a drive. Bear left on this, past another house and out towards the road. When the drive swings sharp right towards a pylon, a corner can be cut by going straight ahead, over the brow of the field to approach a church just ahead. From an intervening wall-stile cross to a stile onto the road, just left of the church.

Coke ovens, Broadhead Clough

St. Mary's Mission Church, Grimehills carries a stone tablet stating *Trinity Church Sunday School, Over Darwen, 1851.* The road along here is on the line of a Roman road, linking the fort at Manchester with that at Ribchester in the Ribble Valley. Look across it to see the spoil heaps resulting from excavations for Sough railway tunnel: an airshaft can be seen a little further left. **Turn left down the road the few yards to the handily placed *Crown & Thistle* pub.**

At the end of the pub car park a rough road runs down to the right to Whittlestone Head. This small hamlet clusters above the southern exit of the Sough railway tunnel. **As the main track swings right, go straight ahead past some stables and a house, to another house in front. Pass round the back and the drive heads away to a fork. Here keep left, straight on past the colourful railway tunnel entrance.** Sough tunnel was completed in 1848, and carries the Blackburn-Bolton line for 2015 yards beneath the environs of Cranberry Moss.

The pleasant track runs on over two small, intervening side cloughs. After the second, turn up the fieldside and rise above an overgrown sunken way to the field top, finding a stile on the right just before the end. Alternatively, keep on towards Cote Farm, then at the cattle-grid take a thin path up to the right to rise to the stile.

Through the stile, rise with the fence and another sunken way on to a stile at the top. From it go left in line with yet another abandoned old way. At the time of research, a Countryside Stewardship footpath offers the option of keeping straight on to enter the old quarry ahead, then following the track through the centre to rejoin the main route. **At a stile on the right where fence meets wall, the sunken way curves round a fieldside to join a broad track on the edge of the heather reclaimed quarries of Edge Fold. Keep on to join a rough road at the end.** For a return to the *Strawbury Duck,* simply turn left on here to be at the bar within ten minutes.

For greater interest take the gate/stile on the right and head off down the old road. In the first dip take a stile on the left and a path descends an old walled way through the trees. Emerging, it continues down to a wall corner, then swing left on a path slanting down towards the plantation enclosing Entwistle Reservoir. It enters the trees to join the shoreline path. To add on a further easy 1½ miles, turn right here and encircle the reservoir. **The obvious return goes left the few minutes out onto the road, then cross the embankment to conclude.**

LOG OF THE WALKS

WALK	DATE	NOTES
1		
2		
3		
4		
5		
6		
7		
8		
9		
10		
11		
12		
13		
14		
15		
16		
17		
18		
19		
20		
21		
22		

SOME USEFUL ADDRESSES

Ramblers' Association 1/5 Wandsworth Road, London SW8 2XX
Tel. 0171-339 8500

West Pennine Moors Countryside Service
Great House Barn, Rivington Lane, Horwich, Bolton BL6 7SB
Tel. 01204-691549

Lancashire Countryside Service
Planning Dept, PO Box 160, East Cliff County Offices, Preston PR1 3EX
Tel. 01772-264709

Clough Head Information Centre
Clough Head Quarry car park, Grane Road, Haslingden, Rossendale
Tel. 01706-830162

Great House Barn Information Centre
Rivington Lane, Horwich, Bolton BL6 7SB   Tel. 01204-691549

Jumbles Information Centre
Waterfold car park, off Bradshaw Rd, Bradshaw, Bolton Tel. 01204-853360

Roddlesworth Information Centre
next to the Royal Arms, Tockholes Road, Tockholes, Darwen
Tel. 01254-704502

Tourist Information Centres
Town Hall, Blackburn Road **Accrington** BB5 1LA Tel. 01254-386807
King George's Hall, Northgate **Blackburn** BB2 1AA Tel. 01254-53277
Town Hall, Victoria Square **Bolton** BL1 1RU Tel. 01204-364333
The Met Arts Centre, Market Street **Bury** BL9 0BW Tel. 0161-7055111
41/45 Kay Street **Rawtenstall** BB4 7LS Tel. 01706-226590

Lancashire County Information Centres
15/17 Railway Road **Blackburn**   Tel. 01254-681120
55/57 Union Street **Chorley**   Tel. 01257-241693
Kay Street **Rawtenstall**   Tel. 01706-213677

Transport Information
Lancashire: County Surveyors Department, Lancashire County Council,
Winckley House, PO Box 9, Cross Street, Preston PR1 8RD

Greater Manchester Passenger Transport Executive (Bolton/Bury areas)
9 Portland Street, Piccadilly Gardens, Manchester M60 1HX
Local bus and rail information: Tel. 0161-228 7811

National Rail Enquiries Tel. 0345-484950

INDEX

Principal features: walk number refers